Background Acting Secrets: How to Become A Movie Extra Today

Find out the inside scoop on how the industry works and how you can be on TV shows, in commercials, and even movies.

Deacon Ford

www.BackgroundActorSecrets.com

Any examples of income are for illustration purposes only. State and Federal laws regarding minimum income levels are subject to change. Nothing in this book is a guarantee of income. Some examples use estimates which are for illustrative purposes only. Nothing in this book should be considered legal or accounting advice. If you require legal or accounting advice, contact a licensed attorney or accountant. This book is based on the personal opinion of the author and his experiences and does not necessarily represent the beliefs or policy of the publisher, Elite Minds Inc. Any mention of specific companies or websites is not necessarily an endorsement. Please be aware that websites can change ownership so any websites listed in this book may be different than the sites that were originally listed. The contents of this book are based on the personal opinion and experiences of the author.

Background Acting Secrets: How to Become A Movie Extra Today

ISBN13: 978-0-9845361-0-8

©2010 Elite Minds Inc., All Rights Reserved

No part of this publication may be reproduced, stored in a retrieval system or transmitted in any form or by any means, electronic, mechanical, photocopying, recording, scanning or otherwise, except as permitted under Sections 107 or 108 of the 1976 United States Copyright Act, without the prior written permission of the Publisher.

All trademarks are property of their respective owners.
You can find more useful educational material at

http://www.EliteMindsInc.com/shop/

How You Can Work As A Background Actor(Extra) in Movies, Commercials, and Television

Introduction

Have you ever wanted to be on TV or in the movies but lacked acting experience? Background acting takes zero experience and you do not even need any Hollywood connections(other than me)! Background acting is also great for actors who have trouble finding regular acting jobs. Background acting is where many actors get started and how they pay the bills until their acting career takes off. It is also how many average people find a little excitement by participating in the entertainment industry.

I will reveal the world of the Movie Extra to you.

I worked as a background actor(also called an Extra) for over three years. A small sample of the jobs I worked are listed in the appendix along with some famous people I met in the industry. This book documents almost everything I learned and in it I reveal the secrets that will help you succeed in Hollywood.

Now, let's get you started in the movie business.

What is an Extra?

Extras, also known as a background actors or background talent are the people who never talk and are usually out of focus on TV and in movies. These are the people walking down the street, eating in a restaurant and the people riding in the bus. The crowds, the reporters at a boxing match in a commercial, the spectators in a courtroom, they are all extras.

There are a number of agencies that manage background actors. You never apply directly with a studio or with a production company to work in a production. They do not keep track of background people. When they want background actors for a commercial, TV show, or movie, they call a special agency that will provide the number and variety of actors needed. I will go into more detail about these agencies and how you can sign up with them later.

Why be a movie extra?

There are various reasons people want to do background work.

- *First Step to Acting or Other Film Work* - Being on set gives you the chance to meet people. Not just crew but other extras who have their own independent projects, skills and ideas. You can also meet big name actors. Make friends with the film crew. Any one of them may be working on another project in a different capacity(like casting or director of photography). If the crew likes you, then you might find a job through them the next day or even months later. I once worked on a commercial where I was upgraded to a principal. Months later the director specifically requested me to play the part of a prison guard in a new commercial. You never know who will remember you or what job they may have available later. The person who works as a production assistant today may be working as casting director or sound engineer on another job tomorrow.

- *First Step to SAG card.* - SAG is the Screen Actors Guild, The Actors Union. Not just anyone can join SAG. One of the easiest ways to join is to work on a union shoot. SAG members work less but get paid more and have higher profile jobs available. To become eligible for SAG membership you have to obtain three SAG vouchers or work as a principal in a SAG signatory production(a production that has a contract with SAG where they agree to hire a certain number of SAG actors). I will explain this in detail later.
- *Generate Part Time Income* - If you do not have a regular job or do not work regular hours, you can work as a background actor. It gives you something fun to do and generates some extra income.
- *Fun in and of itself* - Working as an extra allows you to do lots of things and see lots of events most people never see or do. It is always fun to watch a commercial on TV and say "I'm in this" or to drive down the street and reminisce to a friend about the time you made a commercial in that building or shot a movie on that corner.

I do want to let you know at the start that Los Angeles is the center for background actors. There are jobs in New York and other areas, but LA is where you are most likely to find work and it is where my career started. I will cover resources in the appendix you can use to find jobs in other areas too.

PREPARATION

Before you do anything, especially before spending your money or quitting your regular job, read this next section.

Availability

Extra work requires you to be available on short notice. Frequently you will be called on Monday afternoon to work on Tuesday at 6AM. This means having another full-time job can be a problem if you are thinking of doing background acting on the side.

If you have a full-time job and cannot take off when you want, then you will never be available for extra work. Weekend jobs are prized because they pay more. They go to regular background people with established histories and SAG people so you are not likely to get any weekend work.

FIRST STEP -Signing Up

Before I tell you how to sign up with background agencies, I want to warn you about some common scams that target people looking for background acting jobs.

Penny Ads Scams

You have probably seen these advertisements in the free or paid newspapers offering "Extra Work $300-$600 per day." Now, I am not saying every one is necessarily a scam but... Have you called these? What did they want? $200, $400? Sometimes they want you to pay an outrageous sign-up fee or want you to sign-up for headshots or acting lessons at their school. They are just out to make money off of you. You should never have to pay more than $40 to sign up anywhere.

Headshots/Acting Lessons
Any background talent agency that wants you to take acting lessons or sell you headshots at a specific place promising background work if you do what they say is trying to scam you.

Not over $40.
If anyone wants over $40 as a sign-up fee, you can suspect they are making money from you not making money for you. You do not have to spend a lot of money to work as a background actor. The same applies to modeling and acting. You should make money not spend it. It is true that many legitimate companies charge a sign-up fee. This keeps away anyone who is not serious and helps to pay their bills. It is simply how things are done in Hollywood. Some agencies charge a monthly fee, but you should see regular work before the end of the first month with these companies. You will then know whether or not they are worth paying for another month.

Internet Websites
There are many websites promising background acting jobs and all you have to do is sign up. It is free. Or is it?

When I first decided I wanted to do background acting I signed up for all of the free websites. It was a total waste of time. Sites like moviex.com and free sites like hollywoodweb.com never got me a single job. Most of these free sign-up sites are only used when a production needs many extras, in the hundreds. Don't waste your time with these places. Most of them only want your email to market to you which means spam you. Never trust any online only site that charges a $12.95 sign-up fee either. They make money charging fees and never have to deliver anything for it.

Monthly Fee Sites
Some websites charge you a monthly fee to post your headshot. Usually, the only people who will ever see your headshot at these sites are other extras considering signing up. REAL casting directors rarely go to most these sites. They have no reason to use them, they cast from their own files or from established actor sites. There are some legitimate sites where you can post your headshot, reel, and information if you are an actor or background actor. You will have to ask fellow background actors which sites they like. The top sites change all of the time. They will tell you which ones are the best sites and get you work. Smaller independent productions and some larger casting companies as well as the single person casting companies use these sites so they are not all bad. Some are used by casting companies and others are not used at all. It is one of those things where you just have to dive in and find out which sites are the current top sites and which are not. There is nothing wrong with signing up at the low ranked sites, just do not give any personal information(like your social security number) to them and if anyone calls you because of the posting, verify they are legitimate and always take a friend to your first job.

$5 Listing Websites
There are a number of websites promising: "Sign up online for $5 and we will add you to our database" These are total scams. You will never be called. There are rumors about some big 1,000 person calls actually using them once in a blue moon but you would never want to work one of those calls anyway.

Legitimate production companies only deal with casting companies they know. They all have a list of casting companies they like and those are the ones they call when they want actors or background actors. Production companies no longer have large cattle calls either. Today, they use digital crowds. That means they film empty seats in a stadium and fill them up with digital people, or they sample 20 to 100 real extras and digitally copy them to the other seats. These kinds of websites promising free sign-ups or $5 sign-ups are a waste of your time. You also want to make sure you NEVER give your social security number to any of these free or $5 sites. If you do sign up at one, and someone calls later asking personal questions or asking for your social security number, do not give it out. You can always provide it to the production company on set if it is a real job and really needed for tax reasons. You never have to give it by phone.

Now for the real and legitimate companies.

There are other books that go into great detail listing the companies with their current needs and contact information. This information changes so I will not try to reproduce it here. You can find a list of recommended books in the appendix. This book is meant to help you find a job and do it well plus explain what to expect on set so you are prepared and professional. This book is not a list of contact information. That requires a full book itself and the books in the appendix have that information.

Legitimate companies usually require you to fill out a form and many ask for a sign-up fee of $40 or less. These are called background talent agencies. There are two other services that you also want to know about. One is a calling service, which we will discuss later. The third company is somewhere in between. These are background agencies that charge a monthly fee which is less than a calling service, they do not guarantee any jobs, but do work with a select pool of people they hire regularly. If you can get in this group for a big agency, you can work fairly regularly.

There are some items you will need to be employed as a background actor. No one cares about your acting history or past work history. There is no background check and no eye test either. They care about your look and your sizes. If a company needs 30 African American people of average size, 40 Caucasian who are over weight, and 10 Asians over six feet tall who can fit in a basketball uniform, that is an order the background service fills. They need to know your height and weight to determine if you are average or oversize. They also want a good photograph so they can tell what you look like.

Headshots and 3x5's
A headshot is a professional photograph, usually black and white, on 8x10 glossy paper. Background actors do not need headshots. There are many photographers in Los Angeles who offer headshot services. If you are an actor or model, you will need a headshot, but not if you are a background actor. You can use a headshot too, but you will want to use it along with your 3x5 photo.

Background actors use 3 inch by 5 inch photos instead of headshots. Usually men are photographed in Suits and women in a dress or something dressy. The majority of calls are for business wear or dressy-casual so casting directors want to see what you look like in something dressy. Those are the looks you want to promote. Dress your age. If you are in the 18 TLY(to look younger) range you may not want to dress in a suit but something more appropriate for your age.

Specialty Looks
If you have a special look, like a biker look, then take a

photo in that outfit as well as in a suit. Never take your 3x5 in jeans or shorts. That will not help you get work. If you have a special skill that involves an outfit, take a photo in that outfit. If you are a professional clown, that would make a great photo. If you worked as a nurse and have a nurse outfit, take a photo in it. Pull together a decent wardrobe without spending much money.

If you are someone who looks like Santa Clause with a real beard, that can be a great advantage. There is a demand for Santa Clause look-a-likes year-round and they are paid well. If you work in background acting and make it known you can play Santa Clause, it may help you get those specialty jobs.

Thrift Stores

Thrift stores are a great way to add to your wardrobe. At $2 and $5 per item, shirts are practically disposable. It is much better to get a cheap but nice looking suit from the thrift store to work background than to use your own expensive suit. The thrift stores in Ventura, California are some of the best for selection and prices. It is worth the drive from LA to walk down main street in Ventura and check out the major thrift stores on that strip. You can also find uniforms and tuxedos at the Ventura thrift stores for good prices. Having a tuxedo can help you get a job, just make sure you take a 3x5 of you wearing the tuxedo.

At first, you may be tempted to load up on costumes and wardrobe. Avoid that temptation. Having a huge wardrobe will not help you get work. If you have the right look, you will be hired. The only clothing that can help you are a nice suit(or women's business suit), a tuxedo(or cocktail dress), and a police uniform. So, don't buy every costume you can think of and hope that maybe it will help you get hired.

You will only be wasting your money. If you have a special skill, like being a party clown, that is useful because of the skill, not the outfit. Simply having a clown outfit may not be helpful because if anyone can wear an outfit, then the production company will make their own arrangements for costumes. They will not hire you just because you have a clown outfit.

Don't go overboard with costumes and props. They may help you if you are working no-budget movies for your friends, or you want to do low budget movies just for experience and plan to buy your way in with a wardrobe, but any commercial production will have already budgeted for a construction worker get-up or a priest outfit from a costume company. Having these will rarely help you and it will always cost you money. Don't do things that cost you money. If you have a karate uniform, list it on your information sheet and take a 3x5 photo in it, but do not buy one in the hope you will get a job because of it.

3x5 Photo Format
The 3x5 photo is the calling card of the background artist. The 3" by 5" is from your waist up against a WHITE background. It should be evenly lit with no heavy shadows. It is not a photo of your dog and should not show your favorite motorcycle in the background. It is not a photo from last Christmas either. It is just you, looking professional in a suit(or dress) or in your costume.

Do Them Yourself
Use your own digital camera with a timer to take your photos. There is no need to pay a professional for 3x5 photos. If you want to do serious commercial work, you will need nice 8x10 headshots that are professionally made. For background work, start out small and see if you need headshots later. Use

the camera timer or have a friend take several photos and see which one comes out the best. Then print 20 or 30 copies of that photo. This is what you will send to the background casting companies.

Beware of making your own headshots. You can make your own 3x5 shots, but unless you are an experienced photographer, do not make your own headshots. Digital cameras and quality home printers make it easy to take your photo and print it out. These do not always look as good as they should and if you do not have a photographer's eye, you may not see the problems that are in your photo. If you need headshots, pay a professional, get the minimum number of shots, scan one, and then you can print them out yourself if you need more. You can also ask the photographer for a digital version of the photo.

On the back of EVERY photo put your NAME, PHONE NUMBER, and MEASUREMENTS, as well as your car information. If a CD(casting director) pours out a box full of photos for the Director and he picks one he likes, what happens when they have no idea who it is? That's right, it is tossed back in the box and they pick someone else. Always include your name and contact information on the back of every photo.

Information Sheet

You will also need an information sheet. A sample is shown in the appendix. You do not need a formal resume or an actor's resume. The information sheet is all you need for background work. List anything that could be useful for casting companies.

Some casting companies will accept this sheet as it is and

some will want you to fill out their form. Either way this is a critical piece of information that you must have. You will need your sheet to fill out the form of the background agency. Always take extra copies too. You never know who you may meet at the casting agency who can also provide you work.

Your information sheet should include your:
- Name - Your real name or screen name if you are in SAG.
- Address
- Phone number(s) - Including cell phone number so they can reach you anytime. Does anyone have a pager anymore? If so, you can include that.
- Qualifications (keep it very short)
- Measurements - These measurements are very important because many background actors are cast based on whether or not they fit the wardrobe or if they are taller/shorter than the star.
- Special Skills - If you have any special skills list them. These are very, very important and can determine if you get specialty pay or not. If you can walk on stilts, fold balloons into dogs, breathe fire, ride a motorcycle, scuba dive, are a trained gymnast, dancer, waiter, bartender, or anything else, list it and make sure it is clear to the casting company.
- Union Status - Put your union status clearly on the sheet. If you are a member of the Screen Actors Guild then you are Union (SAG), otherwise you are Non-Union. Your options are Non-Union, SAG, AFTRA, SAG & AFTRA.

How-to-Measure Information for Men and Women
- For Women's Hips — Stand with heels together and measure around the fullest part of hips.
- Hat - Use a cloth tape or string to measure around the largest part of the head starting 1" above the eyebrows.

Divide the inches by pi(3.14) to get your hat size. Round to nearest 1/4"
- Inseam— Take a pair of pants (not jeans) that fit you well. Measure (to nearest inch) from the crotch seam to the bottom of pants.
- For Chest/Bust Size — Measure just under the arms, completely around the back and across the broadest part of the chest area. Hold tape level all around(parallel with the ground).
- Belts — Measure belt 2" larger than your waist size. If between "even" sizes, use the next larger size which is an even number.
- Neck — Measure a shirt that fits you well. Lay the collar flat and measure from the center of the collar button to the far end of the button hole. The number of inches equals your size. You can also measure your neck with string. Place two to three fingers between your neck and the string to give some breathing room.
- Gloves —Measure around your hand at fullest part (exclude thumb). The number of inches equals your glove size.
- Sleeve — Measure from the center of the collar (in the back), across the shoulder and down the sleeve. Number of inches equals sleeve length.
- Shoe Size - look at the bottom of your shoe or inside on the sole.

If you do create a resume, here is some general advice and mistakes I have seen.

Don't pad your resume too much. In Hollywood, everyone knows you can work as a PA or even Director of Photography on a $100 budget movie and put the credit on your resume. Unless the movie has won an award that people have heard of, don't list more than a few credits like this. This kind of credit will not help you in background work anyway.

> *I once worked on a job with an actor who studied acting at Harvard. He said he was considering taking it off his resume because he did not think anyone believed him. So many people lie on acting resumes that it sounded too good to be true. It did not matter anyway because no one was impressed by it. In Hollywood, actors are hired for what they can contribute to the production, not for any training or experience at big name schools.*

Wardrobe – list anything you have that could be used, suits, tuxedo, dresses, etc. Do you have a police officer uniform, fireman's uniform, nurse uniform? Put it down. Anything you can think of that is unusual should be listed.

Props - List any special prop you have like a mountain bike, motorcycle, roller blades, sports equipment, guitar, trumpet, stilts, all of these are needed from time to time.

Car - List the type of car you have, year, make, model, condition and include a photo if you can. When a scene requires many vehicles, the production company often uses the cars of background actors. If you have ever seen a movie with a highway full of abandoned cars or a scene in an intersection where all of the cars are stopped, those were more than likely cars owned by the background actors. If your car is used on set it can mean some extra money at the end of the day. Production companies may want a fancy sports car or an average economy car. All types are used in the background.

Experience - If you have taken acting classes or have experience that can be helpful, then list it. If you have scuba certifications, you attended clown college, you worked in a circus, you race motorcycles, or any other experience, list it. Somewhere, some company needs several background actors who can ride a motorcycle or who can suit up for a scuba diving shot. If you are an amputee, make sure you list this. Jobs that require amputees pay a premium rate.

Avoid listing specific commercials. If you worked a Bud Light Beer commercial then you may be passed over for a Coors Beer commercial or an anti-alcohol public service announcement if they see the Bud Light commercial on your info sheet. They will never ask if you were visible in the commercial, they will simply pass you over. It is best to list commercials you have appeared in as "Available on Request". Sometimes companies need this to make sure there will be nothing embarrassing (like having the same person featured in a competitor's ad), but they rarely request it.

Don't list the names of companies on your information sheet.

If you have extensive experience, it is better to list it on a separate page for acting jobs. Lots of experience does not matter for background jobs. If you are getting started then you are likely just padding out the page so it does not look empty at this point so you can put it on your main page if it is not too crowded.

Age - Give your real age. There is no need to lie to the casting company. They will lie for you if they are doing their job. If you are 33 and look 25 they will send you on a casting call for 18-25 year olds if they can. If you lie about your age and say you are 25 when you are 33, you may not be considered for a job requesting a pretty 30-35 year old woman.

Ethnicity -Tell the truth about your Ethnicity. Just because you think Caucasians get the majority of work is not a reason to list yourself as White if you are really half White and half Hispanic. Put down what you look the most like. If you look Hispanic and put Caucasian, then when the casting company searches for the keyword Hispanics in their database trying to find 100 Hispanics, they will never see your file come up. When they look for 100 Caucasians and your Hispanic face pops up, they will pass it over because you are not what they need for that job. You will be cutting yourself out of a lot of jobs. List your Ethnicity as what you really look like.

Correct Phone -Be sure to give the correct phone number. Many people give bad phone numbers or move and change their phone number and then complain that they never get any work. Give your cell phone number and home phone. I don't know of anyone who still uses a pager, but if they ask for a pager number, give your cell number if you do not have a pager. If a casting company needs someone right away they may not leave a message on your home answering machine. If you do not have a cell phone, you will need one for this business.

Those are the important points that should be on your information sheet. You can also see an example in the appendix.

Don't get your profile marked as "DO NOT USE".

Never register with a casting company and tell them you can only work Tuesday and Thursday after 9AM blah blah blah. They will say thank you, accept your sign-up fee and mark your file as DO NOT USE. They simply cannot use you if you are only available at limited times. They need people they can call on a moment's notice and people who will show up reliably when they are hired. When a casting company needs 100 people the next day, they do not have time to call you and see if you can maybe show up or if the job fits YOUR schedule. They will not bother calling and will call the next person on the list who is listed as available *Anytime*.

Your Website
It is a good idea to have your 3x5 photos and bio on your own webpage. Not a Facebook page or any other social networking site. You need your OWN webpage at your own domain, not a sub page on your Internet providers site. You may be talking to a casing director on the phone and find out they are seeking a look that you can provide, but the casting director does not have the photo of you in your biker gear. If you have a website somewhere you can give him the link and he can see your photo and maybe get you a good job right away. I have talked to a number of casting directors who only had one photo of me and needed to see me in my LAPD uniform which I had on my website. I gave the CD my link and got a job. The url should be something easy to understand and it should be clear.

SIGNING UP

If you want to work as a background actor you must let background casting agencies know you are available and interested.

Sign Up In Person
You have to sign up in person for some casting companies, but others will accept sign-ups by mail. This is changing today and more are allowing online sign-ups. You can find the addresses and sign up procedures for casting companies in the books listed in the appendix.

You should show up on time if you schedule a sign-up

appointment. Not excessively early and absolutely not late. Bring multiple copies of your 3x5 photos, your information sheet and a photocopy of your driver's license, your social security number and a pen. If you are not an American citizen then you will need to bring your passport and green card or work permit too. If you do not look American or have an accent, it is a good idea to bring your US passport in case the agency is unsure whether or not they should hire you.

Fees

Fees are part of the sign up process. Some companies do not require a sign-up fee but most do. You should definitely submit to all of these free agencies since they are free. The industry average is $25 but is growing to $40. There is no guarantee they will use you at all even after making this payment. If anyone wants to charge you $100 or more, you should make sure they are legitimate before paying anything.

Some companies prefer to take their own photos and call the registration fee a "photo fee". Anyone who charges over $40 should be passed over. Agencies that charge a monthly fee should offer some kind of guarantee, such as if you do not work at least twice then you get the next month free. There are legitimate agencies and calling services that charge $50 and even $200 a month. You will have to identify which are legit and which are just after your money. Any agency that makes big promises to get you to write a check should be avoided. One of the biggest warning lines is when they say "I have a job you would be perfect for on our lines now, all I need is your sign-up fee of $200". This line is used to pressure people into signing-up thinking jobs will come easy. This person may get a single minimum wage job but then no more. Then after the month is over, the person gets a call saying the casting company has a job but you must renew your membership to get the information. I will talk about some of the good and bad later.

Acting Classes
If any company insists you sign up for their acting classes or for some other company's acting classes then get out. They are in the business of selling acting classes and you are wasting your time.

Calling Services
Another way to find work is to use a calling service. A calling service charges you a monthly fee and they actively pursue work for you. The fee is usually around $65 to $100 per month. The calling service keeps in contact with casting companies and when they find work for you, they accept then they call you and tell you when and where you are working. They do not usually ask if you are available or interested, they simply tell you where to go because the job is already set up.

Extras Management is the calling service that does the majority of TV related work and they are connected to *Central Casting* which has a virtual monopoly on TV casting work. Ask other extras who their calling service is and who they recommend. Finding a good service that accepts new clients is very much a word of mouth affair. A calling service that was good last year may not be doing as good of a job for it's members this year. The business is always changing.

Can companies charge a percentage? Unfortunately they can. It is not always a bad idea. Those companies have even more incentive to get you work when they make a percentage of what you earn. Which would you prefer, working 54/8 (meaning $54 for 8 hours in background actor lingo) with no percentage paid to the casting company or working 150/10 and paying the casting company 15% If the company is getting you work and you are making decent money it can be worthwhile. When you find one of these companies, you must quickly determine if they are worth working for or not. Do not keep paying a monthly fee or accept one job a month from them if you are not getting enough work. They either get you enough work or they do not. If they do not, never hope that somehow things will change next week or next month.

Big Boys
When you are new to this business you do not know who the big companies really are. Who do you sign up with? Go through the books listed in the appendix and they will tell you who the major players are.

I will give you some highlights here.

Central Casting is the major TV casting company. You will do a lot of work for a trivial amount of pay but it is TV which means a lot of work is available. Some of the jobs are as audience filler(I will explain what Audience Filler is later).

Here are some of the big players in the background industry:
- Bill Dance
- Axium Casting
- Sande Alessi Casting
- Landsman/Kaye Casting
- Extra Extra
- Jeff Olan Casting
- Background Artists
- Background Players
- Background Talent Services(They charge $25/month but are a good company if you do a good job.)

Others....

- Headquarters Casting(spin off of HOS - Hollywood Operating System) See the appendix for more information on this company.
- Unlimited Casting(uses various names and posts on telephone poles, charges outrageous sign-up fees with big promises) -Not recommended

Which Casting Services should I avoid?

Avoid any casting company that wants to charge you over a $40 one-time fee to sign up. Avoid any casting company that wants any large up front fee or wants you to pay for multiple months in advance to get a discount. If you find out that they are lousy they already have your money. Avoid any casting company that requires you to take any classes or to get photos from their photographer or from a list of their approved photographers(which all give the agency a 50% kick back or else they are all the same photographer with different company names). This school or photographer is usually directly connected with the company and you will wind up paying for something you do not need. Avoid any company that advertises on telephone poles. Avoid any company that puts up printed signs outside of other casting agency offices. Avoid any company that runs ads in free newspapers. Avoid any company that says they have a job for you now if you just sign up or if they say they have a job for a *fill in your description here* on their lines that would fit you exactly based on the description which not coincidentally matches you exactly. They may say they need a pretty African American female around 150 pounds and you would be perfect, and when the next person walks in to sign-up, they have a job for a seven-foot tall man with a beard on their lines **right now**...what a surprise. Whatever you are, they will always have a job already on their lines if you will only pay the sign up fee. These are all clear signs of dishonest agencies that you should avoid.

When you pay your sign-up fee, pay in cash. Never give your credit card number. If you use a service that charges a monthly fee, then make an excuse and say you will call later with your credit card number. Go home, go to the website of your credit card company and generate a virtual credit card number. Set the time limit and charge limit. If you later find out the background agency is useless or not getting you jobs, you can cancel the virtual card easily so they will not be able to keep charging you a monthly fee. If you have a problem then cancel your virtual card BEFORE contacting them to cancel your service. Canceling the virtual number first will prevent them charging you for the following month early and then claiming no refunds.

Casting companies are supposed to be making money by farming you out. Anyone who tries to sell you anything or get your cash up front is scamming you whether they are a casting company, website, or any other service that promises to get you work.

> *When I first started extra work I had no idea what I was doing or who was legitimate. I responded to a listing in a local free newspaper classified (which was a mistake, never respond to any casting or background company that advertises in classified ads, especially in free newspapers). The company(I cant give the name but lets just say they were Unlimited in their claims) told me exactly what I wanted to hear, that they had a job on their lines now which I would be perfect for and they could keep me busy. All I had to do was pay a $200 a month sign-up fee so I did. They got me a total of TWO jobs. Both were audience sitting jobs, one for $54 and the other for $25 cash. They never*

contacted me again during my membership. The day before my membership expired, they called again and wanted to book me on another audience sitting job if I renewed. By this time I was older and wiser. It was a pure scam that targets people new to the extra business. There are several such companies. They change names and addresses often and one company can operate under several names but always use the same methods: advertising in classified ads, on light poles, and outside of other casting company offices, then they want a big up-front payment. It's a scam, avoid these kinds of companies.

What if I have been scammed?

Never let a scammer keep your money. Every time you file a complaint with your credit card company it costs the scammer money and the more complaints against them the more likely they will have their credit card service shut down. Using a virtual card as previously described allows you to easily file a chargeback without having to cancel your card.

File a complaint with your credit card company. File a complaint with the local better business bureau. File a complaint with the Attorney General of California. File a complaint with the ISP of any website that has scammed you or of the webhost for the company.

GETTING BOOKED

You have now been to several of the major companies with your information sheet and 3x5 photos. You are signed-up at the major agencies so what happens next?

It varies. Different agencies work differently. If they are the type of service that calls you, they will call you when a job that is suitable for your look is available. If they are the type of service that provides a hot-line, you will call that line several times a day and let them know if you are interested in a listed job. If they are a calling service, they will call you when they have booked you on a job.

Hot Lines
When you sign up with a company that uses hot-lines, they will give you a phone number where they have a recorded message stating the available jobs. You have to call this number to find what is available and then call another number to tell them you are interested. These services are good if you need to earn money and cannot afford to sit and wait for other services to call you. Central Casting has many jobs every day but so many people are trying to get them that it is almost impossible to get through to tell them you want the job. It is best to check the lines very early or very late in the day. Hot Lines usually list jobs and when they are working. If you have a schedule that is not flexible or you work full-time you can use hot-line job listings to find work when you are available. If you have a day off of work or can only work weekends, you can use services that have hot-lines. Hot-Lines allow you to choose jobs you want to work when you are available.

Rejection
Rejection is part of the business. When you do get through to someone about a hot-line listing they may reject you quickly and hang up. This is how the business works. They know what they are looking for and you may not be it. Do not take it personally. They may need someone shorter than you, taller than you, a different race, a different look, anything. Even if you exactly match the description on the hot-line,

they may have already filled that position and not need you for any other position. The information on the job line may not even be correct or they may not know what they want until the right person calls. These background agencies also have many other people to deal with and when you call, someone else is already ringing the other line about another job. The casting director does not have time to chit-chat or to explain why you are not right for the job. He must move quickly and will say yes or no and hang up.

The CD(casting director) does not have time to explain to 100 people why they were not right for a job they thought they were perfect for. When you are accepted for a job or if a CD calls you to see if you are available do not ask 20 questions like "what is the movie about," or "who is in it," or how long does the CD think the day will be. The CD will have no idea what the answer is to many of these questions and will absolutely not have time to explain all of it to everyone booked that day. You have to talk to one CD, but the CD has to talk to 100 people before she can go home for the day. Get your basic information and show up on set. The booking call is to get you to show for a job, not to chat.

If you are accepted for a job then you are said to be booked. That means you have the job and you are expected to show up. If you get another call for another job you have to tell them you are already booked. That is the protocol in Hollywood. You can never cancel a previously booked job because a better one came along. If you do, the agency you cancelled may not use you again. Agencies understand this etiquette and if you say you are already booked they will accept it.

Time and Place Line
The casting company will usually give you another phone

number to call when you are accepted for a job. When you call this number it will have a voicemail message with instructions on where to go, what to wear and what time to show up. This saves the casting director from giving the same instructions to 100 background actors.

If you do not already have a Thomas Guide map book then you should pick up one from any department store. It is a good back-up if your GPS fails. Directions to shooting locations are often referenced to TG(Thomas Guide) pages. Find where you are supposed to go the night before and map it using a service like Google Maps. Also write down all contact numbers and information about the job. The directions may be wrong or it may be difficult to find.

> *A background agency once booked me on a call and gave me the information the night before. I tried to map it then and discovered the directions were wrong. I called the company and the CD confirmed the wrong directions were on the line. Fortunately, she was able to correct the line and contact the people who had already been contacted. Always check the directions, they can be wrong.*

You should know where you are going as early as possible. Do not trust your GPS alone. You should have a printed map too.

Emergency Contact Phone
The casting company usually gives out an emergency contact phone number. This number is for you to call only if you cannot make it to set or you will be delayed or if you have trouble finding the location.

Your casting company has a recorded line for you to use.

Do not call them on their direct line unless they tell you to. They are usually very busy during the day and do not want to answer 200 calls asking "Gee, do you got any work for me" That's what the hot-lines are for! Some Casting Directors work out of their house or from their cell phone. If they happen to call you and you see their number on your caller ID it does not mean you should call that number the next time you need to contact them. It may be their private number or it may not be their number at all, they could have called you from anyone's phone.

What To Wear
Your call information line will tell you what wardrobe to bring. All of the casting companies tell you never to wear solid red, black, or white to the set but integrate those colors into your outfit. The reason they say this is that it causes cinematographers trouble. Those colors stand out too much in a scene. The scene may be all muted colors except for the star. If you wear a white or red shirt, you distract from the star which is never good. You want to blend into the background when doing background work. In practice, there is nothing wrong with these colors. You are usually so far in the background it does not matter. As long as you are not wearing a solid white or red shirt it does not matter, but wear what your casting director tells you to wear and generally choose muted colors.

Take More Than They Ask For
Take at least two changes of clothes. You do not want to wear your favorite blue shirt and find out that five other extras also wore blue shirts. The people in charge of wardrobe will also approve what you have. If it does not match their idea of what should be in the commercial, they will ask you to change into something else you brought. If none of the changes you brought are suitable, you will all be pushed to

the back where no one can see you or wardrobe may give you something else to wear. Bring a change as requested on your information line AND always bring something they did not request. Many times the casting company gets the wrong information and 100 people show up in drab colors when the director wanted everyone in bright happy colors or red-white-and-blue for a patriotic scene. Even if you were told not to bring a red shirt, bring one as a spare anyway. Bring what they ask for and bring something they did not ask for. It just may get you upgraded(promoted to an acting position where you are featured and not in the background).

Specing
Another way to get work is Specing (pronounced specking). To Spec means to speculate. An extra shows up at a job without being booked speculating that they may need more people or that someone who was booked will not show up. If someone does not show up then you may get their job. It is equally likely that you will be turned away. Large jobs may require more people than were booked or they may book less reliable people which means some will not show up. Smaller jobs rarely use specs, but you never know.

There are special mailing lists and calling lines devoted to specing. The resources for these are in the appendix. You can also listen to the recorded hot-lines for a casting company you have signed up with. After you work a job they will usually give a second number with time/place information on the job. Keep this number. They will re-use this number when they have another job. It gives you a way to find out what jobs they are working even if you are not booked on those jobs and you will know when and where the jobs are.

Call this information number for the time and place and show up for the job ready to work without being booked.

Let them know you are specing early. They should add your name to a spec list and if they need one person they will take the first person on the list. Be first.

This will not work if the job is on a major studio lot. Studios have security and if you are not on their list of people allowed into the lot they will not let you in. Specing will only work for jobs that are filmed on location or that are filmed at small studios that are not on the big studio lots.

Be warned that some companies discourage specing. You should only show up for companies that you are registered with.

Rush Calls
A rush call is a last minute call for extras. Someone has a last minute job and needs lots of people to work usually that day or early the next morning. You can find rush calls by listening to the Hot Lines early in the morning 6-11AM, late at night after 7PM, or your calling service may call you at night or early morning.

Cattle Calls
A cattle call means a production company needs a lot of people, hundreds. Most extras learn after the first time to avoid these because they can be long and difficult. The food is not as good and it is crowded. As I already mentioned, there are fewer of these today because big crowds are created digitally.

Audience Work
Television Shows must fill up their audiences. If there are empty chairs then the show looks unpopular. To keep the seats from looking empty(and to have a responsive audience that applauds on command) the studios will hire background

actors to fill the seats. If you stand in front of Grauman's Chinese Theater(Mann's Chinese Theater) from 10AM to 2PM, you can usually find people passing out FREE tickets to shows that will be taping that day. They will give you directions or they may even put you on a bus and take you to the studio right from the theater. The seats they cannot fill for free with tourists, they will pay background actors to fill.

These audience jobs are also the jobs that many low end and even shady background companies pass out after you pay them to become a member. If you sign-up for a background agency and audience jobs are the only jobs you receive, you do not have a good service. These are the lowest paying jobs and are the least fun. Many of the shady background companies get a kickback for every person they supply. This means the person who does the job of sitting in the audience makes minimum wage, around $54 for eight hours, the casting company gets paid an extra $10 to $20 per person directly, and then the background actor may have to pay a percentage or a fee to the background agency. Some of the audience sitting jobs last only two hours, but many can run five to eight hours of sitting to record a one hour show. You can see why they have to pay people for these jobs. Tourists get bored and leave after a couple of hours.

The pay is supposed to be at least minimum wage $54/8(which is $54 for 8 hours of work and you get paid if you are there one second or eight hours and one minute over 8 hours you are supposed to be paid overtime) but is often $25.00 cash paid at the end of the day. This is totally illegal because you are working for less than minimum wage and the casting company is pocketing what you were supposed to be paid. The casting company may keep the extra money plus what they received for booking you plus the fee you paid to sign up. If you are ever offered a job for cash that is less than minimum wage to be in an audience, you know the agency is shady and you should never trust them. Avoid these types of casting companies. If you do the math then you will see why extras learn after the first job not to do this kind of work.

There are times when you can be paid in cash. Small independent films and some super low budget TV programs may pay in cash. These will not be big productions and may be only a director, camera operator, and a couple of actors. The entire crew may be a guy with a camera and a female announcer.

> *I once worked a job for a spot on an MTV program about urban legends. I was told it paid in cash and to go to a certain park. I went there and while I was looking for the crew and trucks I expected to be setting up I met a young girl maybe 18 to 20 years old. She was the producer/director. With her was a camera guy and eventually another actor and assistant joined us. That was the entire crew! We had no film permits, but when you have only a guy with a camera and no lights or fancy set-ups you usually don't need any. We walked into the woods and shot some silly scenes showing the two actors dressed as police officers taking a space alien(the assistant in a mask) into custody. It took about an hour and we were done. I was paid $54 cash. The producer ordered pizza then we sat in the park to eat it under a tree. It wasn't much pay, but it was fun I never saw it on MTV so I do not know if I missed the episode with our segment or if it never aired.*

Even when you are paid cash, it should be at least minimum wage according to state and federal law.

Be Professional

Making movies or commercials is a tedious process. It takes a lot of setup time to get the cameras and lights in the correct positions. During this time the background actor does nothing. Most of an extra's time is spent sitting around and waiting. You can show up at 7AM for a 12 hour job, sit around until 1PM to shoot for 30 minutes, then go back to your holding area where you wait to be released just before your 12 hours are up. This has happened to me on many jobs. There are also times when you are booked for eight hours, show up at 9AM, go to the set immediately and shoot for 30 minutes, then you are released. You get paid for 8 hours and are only there for two or three hours. This too has happened to me many times. Waiting is a big part of the extra's job. You get paid to be available when needed. It is a good opportunity to read. Playing a portable video game or listening to music is common but can also appear unprofessional, especially if you miss a call to the set because of it.

Even when you think no one is watching you, they are. You should always act in a professional manner. When someone is disrespectful to other background actors or acts unprofessionally, the person in charge notices. That background actor may not be booked again or may be put on the 3rd tier list, which means he or she is only called for big cattle calls. Unprofessional actions include sleeping, laying down on the floor as if you are sleeping, bringing a sleeping bag to work with you, and generally lounging around. It simply looks bad and unprofessional when other cast and crew are working hard around you.

I once worked a job for a Bud Light commercial. The background actor's were part of a crowd cheering on two fighting robots. We were supposed to be yelling "Go-go-go" "Fight" "Yeah" and waving our arms.

One of the new extras thought it would be fun to yell whatever he wanted and started yelling "Go Satan, Hail Satan". He thought he was being cute or clever while showing off to the other extras and, since he was in a big crowd, believed his inappropriate actions were unnoticed. He was actually being very unprofessional and was noticed by the experienced extras who were there to do a good job as well as the representative for the casting company. I believe this was his last job because I never saw him at any future jobs with the same casting company.

Food
A good meal can make a bad job much better.

In movies or television production, crafts service or crafty refers to the department which provides food services to the other departments, or "crafts" (camera, sound, electricians, grips, props, art director, set decorator, hair and makeup, background actors).

There is a difference between crafts service and catering. Catering handles the regular hot sit down meals that occur every six hours and usually last between thirty minutes and an hour. Catering is brought in from an outside company hired by the production company or cooked on the spot in catering trucks, but crafts service is a crew position and crafts service people are sometimes represented by the union, IATSE. In Los Angeles crafts service workers are represented by IATSE Local 80 but, in New York, crafts service is a non-union position and is not recognized in the Local 52 charter. Crafts services may provide simple meals or serve-yourself breakfasts, but usually they provide snacks, donuts, fruit and drinks for the crew.

Small jobs usually provide good crafts services and catering. Larger jobs with many background actors are not as well fed. Television shows have really poor crafts-service(food/snacks) for background actors. It is usually a half empty bowl of nuts and a banana on a table covered in crumbs. For TV and movie productions, there may also be different tables with one providing crafts services for the background actors and another for the crew. Small shows with fewer people often have really good food for everyone.

It is not unusual to have steak, shrimp, salmon and other good stuff for lunch on these sets. If you are working a big call of 100 extras then you may only have a cold ham sandwich. Independent productions often skimp on crafts services too. Let crew and cast eat first. Extras eat last.

Production companies are required to feed you every six hours. Sometimes the food is the best thing about the job and many background actors are there as much for the food and conversation as the pay. You must be courteous when it comes to food. Do not fill up your plate when you have a buffet style feed-line. These companies budget a certain number of meals. If you get an extra slice of pizza or a double helping of spaghetti, it means someone on the end of the line gets none.

Sometimes crew and background actors have different meal trucks. Be sure you know which is the one you are supposed to use.

I was once on a job where background actors were supposed to arrive "having-had" which means having eaten breakfast already. This was an early call, around 4AM. About 20 background actors took a free breakfast from the catering truck. The result was that they ran out of food for the crew. Those meals were for the crew and now 20 crew members had no breakfast after they had been there since 3AM setting up. They were not happy.

GETTING PAID

What do you get paid?
When you are starting out you get paid just above nothing. You are hired based on a contracted number of hours. Usually 8, 10 or 12 hours. California minimum wage(at the time of this writing) is $54 for 8 hours which is referred to as 54/8 (fifty four for eight). This is what most non-union people are paid. This is what you get if you work television shows. This is what you are supposed to get if you work audience work. You do get overtime if you work past 8 hours. Time and a half to 12 hours then double time up to 16 hours and past that 16th hour is referred to as Golden Time. Golden Time means you get 1 days pay for every hour or partial hour past 16 hours. Working in commercials often pays more including 150/8 or 250/8 for SAG members. Many days also run long into 12 and almost 16 hours which means you get overtime and that can turn into a much better paycheck.

Productions routinely work for 12 hour and longer days. They will usually try to complete any scenes with background actors to avoid paying them golden time. Remember, when you calculate your time you take 1 hour off for meals.

Bump
A bump means you get a small increase in pay. If you have a specialty or you have a special uniform(not regular street clothes or a suit) you can get a bump for using your own uniform/outfit. You can also get a bump if your car is used in

a scene. You can get a bump if you have to change clothes more than once using clothes from wardrobe.

Screen Actors Guild Pay
SAG members can make 106/8 to start with. You can find the current SAG rates at
http://www.sag.org/branches/sandiego/xtrapay.html

SAG jobs are also harder to get and there are fewer of them available. SAG members sometimes work as non-union even if they are not supposed to because they need the money and it is easier to get jobs as a lower paid non-union background actor.

Taxes And More Taxes
Remember that $54/8 is before taxes. You will have to pay Uncle Sam taxes when you fill out your tax return at the end of the year plus you have to pay for your gas to and from the work site. You usually work in downtown Los Angeles, Studio City, or Hollywood areas. Do not forget to think about your driving time. Always ask "Is it worth the driving time?"

If you are a member of SAG you can get unemployment. Call 1-800-300-5616 They will send you a form and then you wait for your check every 2 weeks. The amount you receive will depend on your income from the previous year.

Actors of any sort are usually unemployed. That is the funny thing about working as an actor or background actor. You are only employed when you have a job for the day. At the end of the day you are unemployed again and have to find a new job. You cannot work one job and expect to file for unemployment. The SAG website will have the latest information on filing for unemployment and the requirements.

Upgrades

You may be lucky enough to be upgraded. When the director decides he needs additional people on camera he will frequently pick someone out of the background actors and upgrade that person to a featured spot. This may mean a few extra dollars or only that you are seen on camera. It depends on the production.

If it is in a union commercial then you may receive thousands of dollars for an upgrade. Union signatory commercials have to pay featured actors every time the commercial is used or is shown on TV. A popular commercial can generate thousands for someone who never says anything in the commercial.

I was upgraded to a featured spot in a commercial. I was moved from the background and all I had to do was look at the primary actor and nod. I received $3000 over the next few months as checks came in every one or two weeks for that one upgrade. Each showed a summary of how many times the commercial was aired. I was expecting to make $150 for the day as a background actor and made $3150 instead.

Always put yourself out front and volunteer for anything. You never know what it may lead to. There have been many times when the AD asked for volunteers to do something less than fun, like to be the background people standing in the scene instead of sitting. I always volunteered for anything that was offered. Sometimes, the AD remembers who volunteered and when a featured position or even a more fun position is available, he remembers the people who volunteered.

I was in the background walking in an office while the two primaries were talking on camera. I had to close a door behind me and knew it would make noise, but I could not act like I was closing it softly because that would be unnatural. Without any direction I closed it as quickly as I could and in the last inch moved very slowly and slowly released the know. At the end of the scene, the director himself turned to me and complimented me on how well I closed the door. Instead of watching the action, he was concerned about excess noise that would ruin the shot. People are watching and paying attention to what you do even when you do not realize it. He remembered me for another scene later. Always pay attention and think about your part in the scene and how to make the jobs of the crew easier.

Sometimes background actors are upgraded to regulars on TV series, like a desk clerk on a police drama or the sceen with a ball-check guy in a bowling alley frequented by the star of a sit-com.

If you are upgraded and are interested in becoming a full-time actor, you should quickly develop amnesia about your background career. Not one director, casting director, producer or writer likes to hear about someone's past background acting experiences no matter how great you think it was. Once you cross the line to be a regular actor, don't look back. If you were ever upgraded to a primary from background, pretend you were originally cast as primary and never tell anyone otherwise.

For some reason the "guys in charge" don't like to hear about their new star's big break because she was making crosses(walking behind the star to give the illusion of a busy street) in a TV commercial. When you become an actor, you were always an actor and never did anything else. Yeah, that's the ticket.

Specialty and Hazard Work

Specialties, like fire breathing, can get you more money too. A parade or circus scene will need many clowns folding balloons or on stilts and jugglers in the background. These people get paid more for their special skill.

If you are working in water or in a hazardous environment you can also receive more pay. BEFORE you are booked for a job you should be told if there will be smoke or nudity on the set(even if it is not you in the buff). You have the right to turn down any such job if you cannot tolerate the fake smoke or if you have an objection to nudity without being labeled as hard to book. You are also supposed to be notified before booking if the job is a night shoot.

LEGAL

SAG Rules cover SAG employees. State Law covers non-union employees. The rules are very similar.

There are a number of employer requirements, but here I will only cover a few items you want to know about: Every extra must be provided with a chair(i.e. they can't dump you on an open field for 12 hours with nowhere to sit). Every six hours you must have a meal break(or get a little extra pay as a penalty). If you work overtime they must pay you overtime (remember that you get one hour off for each meal break). You cannot be paid less than minimum wage.

Rule Violations

What do you do if you see a violation of SAG Rules or California Labor Law? If it is not serious then it is usually better not to make waves. If you make a big deal because your lunch was six hours and thirty minutes after you started work and you didn't get a bump, you may not be asked back by that casting company for any jobs. You will be branded a troublemaker. If you work 10 hours with no meal break and then they just send you home with no extra pay, that would be a very different situation and one where you should complain.

When you first arrive on set you must check-in with someone. That person may be a representative of the casting company or a 2nd AD(Assistant Director) or the first AD(assistant director), or possibly a PA(production assistant). For minor problems you should contact this person first or the first/second AD. If you have a serious problem that does need attention you should talk to the AD diplomatically. If that does not work then you can try the casting company that hired you. Sometimes, if you talk to the AD about a problem, you no longer have a problem, you are a problem. If you have a labor violation complaint or something on that level let your casting company handle it. If they ignore you, then you can move up the ladder to the AD. If you still do not have the problem resolved or at least reasonably compensated you can file a complaint with the state. After all, you have by this time made a good faith effort to resolve the problem. Once you see there is a problem, start documenting everything that is said and done. List on a piece of paper, in your own handwriting what happened, the time and date, why you think it is a violation, what you did as a result, who you talked to, that person's name and job on the set, what the response was, what action was taken if any, and what you did next. This record can be important later especially if any compensation is due to you and other actors. If you are a member of SAG, you can call them right from the set to file a complaint. Who knows, they may even send someone out to the set. You can find SAG procedures on their website. Even if you are non-union, SAG may respond if there are union members on the set suffering from the same violation.

When talking to the AD/CD it is never good to start with "This is illegal" or "I'm not going to put up with this". If you put them on the defensive they will not be willing to help you. It is much better to simply pull them aside and quietly state that you have a concern, and that the labor laws back up your point of view, ask how the situation can be resolved. Many production companies do not know the law and some just don't care.

Determine if your complaint is worth filing. You can file complaints with the California Labor Board if you believe your rights have been violated.
To file a claim visit http://www.dir.ca.gov/dlse/
When is Hollywood hiring?

When is the best time to find work as a background actor or actor? There is usually the most work in January to May then many production people take a summer vacation so most jobs are on hiatus. It usually picks up again in August to December.

Getting to Set

It is your responsibility to arrive for work early enough to find the person you must check-in with. Remember, you may be there with 100 other people so you cannot expect to show up five minutes early and check-in right away. Show up early, have your drivers license with you, avoid traffic, be early. If you are going to a studio then do not bring a pocket knife or anything that will cause trouble at the metal detector.

I once reported for an audience job and there was a

metal detector we had to go through. I took out my metal keys, cell phone, and pocket knife and put it in the tray. Walked through with no problems. Then the security guy said I could not take my pocket knife in the studio. It seemed quite silly to me because my keys were equally dangerous and if I wanted to harm anyone I could push a light over. It was an example of security for the show of security. I asked if he could hold my knife until after the job. He said he couldn't. I thought that was really odd. Common sense tells you that someone out of a crowd of 50 people will have something that they cannot take in and I could not be the only person with a pocket knife either. The security guy did not seem particularly intelligent and had no solutions. I could not take the knife back to my car because it would take too long and we were already being placed for the audience. Finally he had a thought that awakened his brain enough and he said he could hold it until the end of the shoot. I wonder where he got that idea? I picked up my knife on the way out. Never expect common sense to be the ally of security.

Leave your house early enough so you have plenty of time to arrive 30 minutes to an hour early on set. If call time is 9AM for downtown LA then you need to leave much earlier. Get to LA very early. I commonly arrived at 7 AM for a 9AM job. I would park and walk down the street for a leisure coffee near the set. I never had to fight heavy traffic and had plenty of relaxation time before work.

When you arrive at a studio be prepared to go through security which means you will need to allow time for that. Expect a metal detector at any studio and they will pretend to look through your car sometimes too. Make sure you park in an authorized area. Parking in reserved spots can mean you are asked to leave and not come back or be towed.

Showing up an hour early has saved me from many problems. First, if you are early, you get to eat early. If you are early, you can drive in light traffic. If you are early, you can find the location.

> *Once I was supposed to be on set at 7AM. I arrived at 6AM. I apparently turned north instead of south on a connecting street. The north bound lane actually did not go north but east then south. I drove and drove looking for the street and never found it. I checked my map and realized I was far away from where I was supposed to be. I then drove all the way back to find the street. It was a good thing I was early because the shooting location was on was one of those odd LA streets that stops on one block and continues on the other side of a big building. I could not for the life of me find the location no matter how many times I drove up and down the section of the street I was on. Finally, at just before 9AM, I realized the street continued a block away and found the location. This was after I went back and looked at my original directions. I came from the opposite way from what the directions explained. When I re-read them and I was now familiar with the area, it was clear what went wrong. If I had planned to arrive 10 minutes early I would have been very late. I was on time because I tried to arrive early.*

I later bought a GPS system to make finding these locations easier. GPS is not always useful. If you are in the mountains, GPS signals may not always be available. Some of the roads are so close together in the residential areas in the mountains that your GPS can be confused about which road you are on. I was one going to a shoot at a house rented for a movie and had my GPS show that I was driving down a parallel street I was not actually on many times when in the hills and it was giving me incorrect directions such as turn right when there was no right turn. Always print out a map. Never rely solely on your GPS.

On Set
As soon as you are on set find the person you are supposed to check-in with. If it is a big call with lots of background actors, you will likely have a representative from your background agency there who you report to. They may be called an Extras Wrangler. If it is a smaller production with only a few background people, you may report directly to the AD(assistant director) or 2nd AD(second assistant director which is his assistant) or to a PA(production assistant or general helper). This person will give you a piece of paper called a voucher. If you do not have your voucher in your hand then you are not really there and you will not get paid. Keep track of this paper. You will turn it in at the end of the day to prove you were there the whole day.

Get your voucher first before you do anything else.

Vouchers
When an extra goes to a job, he or she is given a Voucher that shows the extra was there, the pay rate and how long he or she worked. The production company(people making the commercial or TV show) hires a payroll company to pay everyone. The extra actually works for the payroll company. Any questions about payments should always be directed to the payroll company listed on your voucher. After you have been in the business a while you will notice that there are certain payroll companies that handle most of the jobs

you work. Start writing down the contact information and names for these companies in case you need to contact them. Payment times vary. Checks are supposed to be mailed in a set time but it is common to take up to 2 weeks to receive payment for a commercial. Work for TV(Central Casting) is usually a quick payment. Work for print ads can take months before you see a check.

SAG Vouchers

SAG(Screen Actors Guild, the actors union) requires a production to hire a fixed number of SAG members for every TV show, Film, or Commercial. These SAG members are given SAG vouchers. By being members of SAG they also get paid more than non-union extras. SAG Vouchers are often called Taft-Hartley's. If a SAG member does not show up the company still has to pay someone as if that person was a member of SAG. Sometimes there are not enough SAG members on set to meet the minimum number. When this happens, the extra SAG vouchers are given to non-union people because they must be used. When you receive a SAG voucher as a Non Union actor you are said to be "Taft Hartleyed". This is a good thing because it means you can now apply to join SAG. Many actors work background hoping to be Taft Hartleyed.

Also, if they need a special talent, like a roller-blader and cannot find a SAG member on short notice who can roller-blade they may hire a non-union background actor. In such a case they give the SAG voucher to a non-union person. This can also occur if the production needs someone with a special costume, like an LAPD uniform, and cannot find an available SAG member.

There are underhanded ways to obtain SAG vouchers, but if you stick with it for a while and don't cause problems they will usually come your way.

SAG members are issued special cards. The card color changes frequently. This makes it easy for a production to glance at a card and know if it is current or not. You cannot gain SAG employment by simply saying you are in SAG. You will be asked for a SAG card to prove you are a member.

Fill out your Voucher and write legibly. If the payment company cannot read your writing, you may not get paid or it may be delayed.

Once you have your voucher you will be told where your holding area is. This is the place you are to stay when you are not actually working on set. When the AD needs you this is where he will look. Not outside by the trees, not in the bathroom, not by your car. He will look in holding and if you are not there you may miss a big opportunity or hold up production if they really need you which may mean this is your last job with this company. Stay in holding until you are needed. Do not wander off or sit in the nearby studio because it is more comfortable. No one will be able to find you when you are needed and you may be asked to leave if you are not available when you are needed.

If the job requires wardrobe approval then you will stand in line so the wardrobe people for that production company can approve what you are wearing. If what you are wearing is not good enough then they will have you change into one of the alternate outfits you brought. If they have you change into something they brought, they will ask for your voucher. They will write what you were given on the back and when you return their clothing you will get your voucher back.

Do what you are told. Be quiet when on set and pay attention.

The Director and other crew have to communicate and it is difficult when the extras are talking. Be quiet, the sooner they get the shot the sooner you can move to the next and maybe make it a short day.

Do Your Job
Never try to do someone else's job. Never help any production crew member with his or her job for any reason. That means no rolling of cables, no moving equipment, no picking up tools, nothing. You should not touch or pick up anything.

The production crews are professionals. They have union rules and procedures. They know their jobs. They do not need anyone to help them. If you are injured while helping them then they have a big problem and a lot of questions to answer like why they allowed you, an untrained bystander, to do their work. Stay out of the crew members way.

Never touch anything unless someone who is authorized hands it to you. This means you do not pickup any equipment and especially NEVER pick up any props for any reason. You can break the continuity between shots or damage a special prop without realizing it. Something that looks like it is metal may be foam or plastic and break easily.

I was working on a TV show and all of the extras were lined up for wardrobe approval. The line extended through the set. One extra a few paces in front of me picked up a script laying on a table and used it as a stiff backer to fill out his voucher. A crew member immediately approached and told him not to pick up anything or move anything. It was embarrassing for the extra, but he should not have touched anything on the set. Someone put that script down and that same someone will expect it to be where it was last placed.

Don't pick up scripts lying around. If someone else put it there then don't touch it. Even trash on set should be left where it is, it may be part of the scene or it may not be trash. If you have any questions about props you can ask the AD or the Prop Master.

Playing Favorites
Background acting is very much an insider job. The best jobs go to a small group of people. You may see these same people at every job you work. You may also think this as the casting director playing favorites. This can be true but it is also how the business works. A casting director finds 50 or 100 background actors who show up prepared, act professionally, and do not complain, plus they are people the CD personally likes. These are the people the CD will use on almost every job. If you can get into this group, you can get many really good jobs. If you are not in this group, you may only get the overflow work or the work these core background actors are unable to take. Eventually, after you prove yourself, you may be in this core group for one CD. If you are in this group, then you may find that you can work almost every day for one background agency.

There are some in-demand people who can get regular work even if they are not in this core group. The 18 TLY(To Look Younger) people are always in demand. These are people who are over 18 but look under 18 and can appear in many high school theme movies and television shows.

Being a pretty girl does not guarantee you work. Hollywood is full of pretty girls. You also need to be very professional and outgoing. Being a pretty girl does help.

Grammar

Using proper grammar is a must. The people who are in charge in Hollywood are smart and educated. If you use words inappropriately, mix singular nouns with plural pronouns or make other grammar mistakes when talking to a CD or director, you will be labeled as unintelligent. This means you may not be considered for featured positions when they come up. You will also meet other extras who have their own projects or know about other movie projects. If you use poor grammar, they may not consider you qualified and therefore will not mention these projects to you. If you use good grammar, you will be viewed as a person who is intelligent and can handle the job. You can find a great grammar video course at
www.SpeakEnglishLikeAGenius.com
This course will help you with your grammar.

Pay Attention

Part of being professional means paying attention. Don't just show up and blindly follow what you are told. Pay attention to the people and things happening around you.

I was once booked on a job where I was very close to the main actress. I wasn't paying much attention. She went through her actions a few times in her pink dress and we cut to setup for the next scene. Everyone went to eat lunch. I was one of the first to get my meal and sat at a table which was empty. A nice girl in a gray sweat shirt who looked like she was part of the crew sat across from me and started talking to me. I was extremely embarrassed when I did not know who she was and I asked what she was working that day. She was not a member of the crew, she was the featured actress I was one foot away from only minutes before. I did not recognize her because she put a sweat shirt over her dress to keep it from being soiled before the next shoot. The rest of our conversation was very short and uncomfortable. Always pay attention to the featured actors. You never know when you will see them again.

Terms You Hear On Set

You will hear some industry terms on set and you should know what they mean. When you arrive on set the assistant director(AD) will place everyone on the shooting location which is your first position and give you instructions on where to walk or what to do.

Reset or Back-To-One means go to the first place you were told to stand and be ready to do your action again.

Camera's Up means the camera is ready, we are about to shoot, make sure everything in the scene is as it should be and you are in your starting position.

Roll Camera, Background Action, Action. This sequence indicates the camera is rolling, background actors should start their activities first, then the featured actors begin their actions. "Background action" means background actors start walking or clapping, whatever they were instructed to do.

Etiquette on the Set
As with any business there are certain social and business rules that apply when dealing with others.

Eye Contact
When doing audience work for interview type shows you should avoid making eye contact with the guests at anytime.

People who are not accustomed to being in front of a camera or crowds can become spooked if one or many strangers are staring at them before the show. Be polite and avoid direct eye contact. The same applies when working with primaries in other productions. When they are giving their lines do not stare at them unless you are told to. If you are out of camera shot you should not stare at the featured actor delivering lines because it can make them uncomfortable. If the scene is particularly intense or emotional you will be making it more difficult for the primary. You should also continue the action you were told to do even if you think you are no longer on camera. You do not want to mess up a scene because you stopped walking and stood still thinking you were out of the camera's range only to find that the camera could see you or the camera moved and you messed up the shot. Always assume you are on camera when action is called.

When doing audience work you should never openly discuss who you work for or how much you are getting paid with other people in the audience. Some of these people are NOT getting paid but have accepted tickets to see the show FREE. If they find out you are getting paid and they are not, it can cause problems. Keep quiet at audience jobs. At the end of the job the free people will be let go and the extras will be kept behind to be paid privately. When the casting company refers to itself it will never say "People for Bob's Casting wait on the bus" they will instead say "People here for Bob wait on the bus" without using the word Casting in front of the unpaid audience members.

Don't make small talk.
The director and crew are busy doing their job. They are always on a schedule and in a hurry. They do not have time to chitchat during filming and need to talk to each other.

Chairs
Extras frequently bring their own fold up chairs. Sometimes this is very nice to have so it is good to keep one in the trunk of your car. They can be a problem in small spaces though. Place it out of everyone's way. If you are in a small room then you should not use one. Your chair should be in a distant corner and not close to any area where many people are walking or where it can block even part of an area where people walk in and out. Be courteous if you use a chair and do not block or restrict walking paths or interfere with other people who do not have their own chairs. Carrying your own chair can also be a problem. Many casting companies do not like seeing extras with their own chairs. They consider it unprofessional. It is too much like lounging on the job. If you have one, leave it in your car and only bring it to holding if you really need it and if there is enough room for it.

Small Talk
Principals are the actors featured in the commercial, television show, or movie. Do not talk to the principals unless they speak to you first. When on set, the star is concentrating on his or her job, they have to hit their marks and get their lines straight in their head. They do not want to chat with each of 50 extras or even 10 of them on the set. They do this every day and it becomes a real burden to have to make small talk with 10, 20 or 100 people every day. That is why you do not talk to the talent unless they speak to you first.

Cameras
You are on set to do a job. You are not a tourist or paparazzi. If you are seen with a camera taking a photo of the star, you may be asked to leave immediately. Taking photos like this, without permission, makes stars, and even non-stars who are featured actors, nervous. I do recommend you take photos, but not of the featured actors. It is always nice to have a

photo album of the jobs you have worked. You can use your cellphone to take a photo of the setup, of the set, of other extras you have made friends with. You are not taking photos of people, but of areas unless you have asked someone if you can take his or her photo. You should not shove a camera or your camera phone in anyone's face though. When you are on set with a big star, just having a camera can result in you being fired on the spot.

Autographs
You are on the set to do a job. You are not a tourist or autograph hound. Taking a book of autographs to set hoping to meet someone famous is inappropriate. Hounding the star or shoving a piece of paper in front of him just before you start filming and asking for an autograph is unforgivable and unprofessional. The featured actor has a job to do and is trying to focus on that job. He does not need 10 or 20 background actors trying to get an autograph in between shots. There are times when famous people will sign autographs on set, but those are rare. Leave your autograph book at home.

Phone
Keep your cell phone off when you are on set. Even in holding it is best to keep it off or at least on vibrate. Your ringer could disturb a scene that you are not in if it can be heard on set. It does not matter if the camera is running or not. No one wants to hear your phone. I say don't even set it to vibrate. People still hear it and it can still be heard on the sound track if it goes off while shooting. A phone going off during filming can get you sent home and the production company may not want you back ever. Turn your phone off when you arrive for work and back on when you wrap for the day unless you are making a call in holding.

In one job I worked a girl had her cell phone stolen. It re-appeared on a table just before the day wrapped. Another background actor stole her phone and used it to make calls all day and then left it on a table. Here's a tip, keep your phone in your pocket and keep it turned off but with the ringer on. If your phone does go missing, borrow someone else's phone and call your phone. If you leave the ringer on but turn your phone off, it will ring if someone else has turned it on.

Myths
Many books on extra work recommend that men put together police uniforms. I have already mentioned this a number of times. Here is the real story. Only put together a uniform if you have it already. Don't believe the advice: get an LAPD Uniform and you will have constant work. It won't happen!

Think about it, how many TV shows and movies have police officers in them? All of them pretty much. It would seem like it is a good idea to have one of these uniforms. It is not. The fact is most TV shows that use lots of police officers already have their own mish-mash of thrown together uniforms or they will hire a costume company and do not care how nice your uniform is or how technically accurate it is. Many casting companies do keep an LAPD file of people with LAPD uniforms. These are commonly requested for SAG jobs where only one or two people are needed or for low budget films that cannot afford the wardrobe fees. If it is a big production they will provide their own uniforms.

I was once hired for a production, Die Mommy Die, because I had a police uniform along with four other background actors. After we arrived with our uniforms, we discovered the production company had their own 1960's police uniforms so we had to change out of our modern uniforms and into their uniforms. At least I got to drive the 1960's police car.

You will be wasting your money if you put out a lot of cash trying to build a uniform. If you are/were a police officer and have a uniform, great and make sure to let everyone know you are an experienced police officer too. If you don't already have one, then don't spend over $50 to put one together. Many extras have fallen victim to this bad advice and spent hundreds of dollars thinking they would be needed every day. For productions that do not have their own uniforms they will call someone from SAG before they will call a NU(non-union) background actor too. Save your money. If you do decide to put together a police uniform, do it cheap. Don't worry about accuracy or a complete accessory belt. A navy uniform shirt and pants with a security guard badge is good enough to make a 3x5 photo. You can often find these on eBay or at thrift stores used and cheap.

San Diego for Vouchers

Many actors become background actors just to obtain a SAG voucher and join SAG. At one time it was easier to get a SAG voucher outside of the LA area. You could work in San Diego or other places where there are fewer SAG extras to increase your odds of receiving a SAG voucher. SAG has changed their rules and controls the number of vouchers more closely so this is not as easy as it once was.

Conclusion

I hope I have answered most of your questions and given you the tools to start working as a background actor in Hollywood or any large city. It is a fun job and allows you to do things few other people have the opportunity to do. I look back on my time in Hollywood with pride and am always happy to talk about the fun times I had.

I hope you will use my advice to get a jump start on your career as a background actor and start having fun too.

APPENDIX A

Books

Extra Work for Brain Surgeons HOS(Hollywood Operating System) Buy this book cheaper used at amazon, not new. It lists many casting companies along with their contact and registration procedures. You also do not have to buy the latest book. Any book will be reasonably up to date. You may also want to purchase the newest version and an older version because some casting company listings mysteriously disappeared in later editions. Use the contact information but do not believe the reviews. It is a good list of casting companies with contact information though.

You can find this book and any others listed at our private page just for people who have purchased this book
http://www.BackgroundActorSecrets.com/private.htm

Movie Extra Work for Rocket Scientists
Another similar book with lots of information and contact listings for casting companies.

Back To One: The Complete Movie Extras Guidebook

Its All Your Fault! by Bill Robinson & Ceridwen Morris (How to be a PA in LA) "*How To Make It In Hollywood*" by Linda Buzzell (where to live, drive, get info., etc.)
Hollywood 101 by Frederick Levy (who does what jobs)

More Advanced Books:

> *Hello. He Lied* by Lynda Obst
> *Wake Me When Its Funny* by Garry Marshall

Which Lie Did I Tell by William Goldman
Making Movies Sidney Lumet
Breaking Into Acting For Dummies
The Truth About Being An Extra

You can find this book and any others listed at our private page just for people who have purchased this book
http://www.BackgroundActorSecrets.com/private.htm

Internet Resources

There is a large community of background actors and featured actors. They can be found through Yahoo groups where they answer questions and discuss the industry.

Useful Yahoo Groups:
http://groups.yahoo.com/group/HollywoodXtras/
http://movies.groups.yahoo.com/group/LAFilmCasting/
http://movies.groups.yahoo.com/group/FilmCastingLists/
http://groups.yahoo.com/group/Agency-ManagementDirt/

These links are also on our webpage along with any updates
http://www.BackgroundActorSecrets.com/private.htm

You can search for other groups at http://groups.yahoo.com Once you locate a group that discusses background actor work in your city, you can follow the discussions to find out what agencies in your area are the best, which to avoid, and how to find good jobs. Many times jobs are posted directly to these Yahoo groups.

Other good websites for jobs:

http://losangeles.craigslist.org/tfr/

http://www.actorsite.com/
http://exithollywood.com/

You can find various low budget and independent crew, acting and background acting job listings on Craigslist.org. Some are unpaid but they can still be fun. As always, exercise caution when responding to any such ad on Craigslist.org and take a friend with you.

mandy.com – a resource for the film industry
la411.com another resource directory

Resource for background actors
http://www.backstage.com/bso/index.jsp

California Labor Board

File complaints with the California Labor Board if you believe a labor violation has occurred.
To file a claim visit http://www.dir.ca.gov/dlse/

Fraudulent Casting Services

I have a detailed story about a fraudulent company that scammed me out of $200. Find out the full story at the website

http://www.BackgroundActorSecrets.com/private.htm

APPENDIX B
Example Information Sheet

John Smith
123 Any Street
Camarillo CA 93010
Home Phone: 000-000-0000
Pager/Cell: 000-000-0000

Union: SAG
Availability: Anytime
Sex: Male
Ethnicity: Caucasian
Height: 5'7"
Weight: 150 lb.
Hair: Black
Eyes: Blue
Birth Date: 04/29/00
Age: 00

Wardrobe:
Karate Uniform
Military Fatigues
Black Leather Trench Coat

Measurements:
Waist: xx"
Jacket: xx
Neck: xx"
Hat: xxx (xxx inches)
Shoe: xxx
Inseam: xx"
Sleeve: xx"
Chest: xx"
Glove: Medium x ¼"

Car: 1990 Corvette, Maroon, Excellent condition.

Acting, and other Film Experience/Training:
Various TV and Film including: X-Files, 24, Die Mommy Die, Rush, Director of Photography for Digital Feature Film "Foolish the Wise"

Special Abilities:
Fire Eating
Motorcycle Endorsement on Drivers License
Paramedic - Nationally Registered EMT-B(Emergency Medical Technician)

Special Props: Roller Blades, Tennis Racket

APPENDIX C
Notable Appearances for TV, Commercials and Film.

The following accounts are from my notes. I highly recommend that you keep a diary of some sort. Many interesting things will happen that you will forget about as time passes. A diary lets you remember these interesting things. Keep notes about the productions you worked on, the people you meet, their contact information, the production companies, the dates you worked, how much you were paid, the fun things you saw, everything! I wish I had taken more and better notes now.

These are truly my rough notes so excuse any grammar errors or any passages that do not make sense. These short stories will help you understand exactly what the work is like and what you can expect in your life as a background actor.

The Best Damned Sports Show
This was my first job and it was audience sitting. We took a bus from the casting company to the studio. Sat there about three hours and that was it. Tom Arnold was nice and talked to the audience. I don't remember who the basketball player was he interviewed. Tom kept a beer behind his chair and sipped it when they were not shooting. The news segment was taped earlier and played during the show as if it were live.

Weakest Link daily series 7/01
This was my second job and the only reason I took the audience job was because I wanted to see the show. Otherwise I would not have accepted $20 cash for the day of 5 to 8 hours. You don't have to be a mathematician to see that is much less than minimum wage and of questionable legality, but that is the common practice. This was filmed in NBC studios. They had ridiculous security measures and even had armed guards lined up as everyone left. I guess it was to make sure no one in the audience ran on the stage. They can shoot them then you know. We were told to wear black so I

wore a nice shirt and black tie. Very spiffy. When we were outside the studio people were staring at us and finally a passer by asked who we were. He thought we were a cult with everyone dressed in all black. After I got inside I saw they rounded up some average people to be in the audience, off the street, and gave them black t-shirts. I had actually never seen the show before so I did not know how much of the audience would be seen. After seeing an episode on tv after I got home I now know that I could have also worn a black t-shirt and blended into the black background. My nice suit and black tie was a waste of time. You can't see anyone in the dark room and the people on the first row are so out of focus it does not really matter what anyone is wearing as long as it is black. The people in front also had to hold a black curtain over their legs. I never figured out why they did not just put up a guardrail or rope and hang the curtain over that instead. During filming the amateurs(free attendees not getting a whopping $20) started to realize why it was difficult to get people to go to these filmings and be in the audience. It is real work and a pain to sit there all day. They would get up to go to the bathroom between takes and then the assistant directors would have to move other paid people in their spots constantly swapping people out to keep the bleachers full. Some of the people were smart and did not come back. We started with 20 extra extras and ended with no spares. This was the last audience job I took.

Bud Light Battle Bots Commercial 08/01- Chelsea Productions, I wore a red shirt as a spectator in all scenes. It was a tough one. We were there right up to 16 hours. A few people stayed longer and got golden time but most of us were released so they did not have to pay everyone golden time. I stayed up all night before the shoot which was a mistake. I learned to get a good night's sleep before work after this.

Dharma and Greg - The principals were attending an imiginary Bonnie Rait Concert. I sat behind the principals in all scenes. They had mirrored mylar on each side of the short bleachers to make it look like a big crowd but there was only a handful of people sitting around the principals. 11/01

Chevrolet/Michelle Kwan Commercial - Chelsea Productions 11/01
Filmed in a skating rink in Anaheim. All of the extras were seated and Michelle Kwan's stand-in was filling her part as they setup the camera moves, focus, and lights. She would skate in a big circle and come to a stop on the ice and hold her arms in a circle out in front where the Chevrolet logo would be placed in post production. We watched the stand-in do that several times and figured out how the commercial worked quickly. We all knew what was going to happen and expected it. Then Michelle Kwan came out. The director called action. She skated around in the circle then to her position, stretched her legs way out and threw her arms into a circle and everyone in the audience went Ooooohhhhh and applauded. It was a huge difference in performance. Truly amazing to see how the stand-in skated and mimed the moves then to see a professional do the same moves with conviction. It was really something to see. We were hired for a 12 hour day and had no reason to expect anything different. After 3 hours of shooting they said "that's it" and sent us home(with 12 hours pay since that was the contract). Not a bad day at all but it was also a 4 hour round trip drive to Anaheim.

Microsoft Stock Trader Commercial - Playing a Stock Trader in a sky scraper, Chelsea Productions. One of the principals was a very outgoing lady. Before we went on set she said "Let's keep it frosty out there" then asked if anyone knew what it was from. No one did. She said it was from Aliens. Since then I have heard the line several times and will never forget it. 12/01

Spin City - outside club goer at Sheen drug arrest 12/01
We were in a line and supposed to look like club goers. The prop handler asked us if we minded holding cigarettes. Then he asked if he could light them as long as no one nearby had any lung issues. We agreed and took fake puffs just in our mouths to test what we would do on camera. Of course, we had to make the joke "Wow, that's good, I will have to pick up a pack of these on the way home". The prop guy was amused. Charlie Sheen smoked like

a chimney between scenes. No one told him there was no real smoking allowed in the studio. It seems stars have different rules.

HR Block Commercial - Accountant, directed by Coen Brothers, Villans Productions 12/01

This was very unusual. I never saw the commercial air. We were all in a big room sitting at identical desks. The idea was that everyone was a mechanical employee who picked up a stack of papers, stamped them put them in the out box, then picked up the next stack and so on. The papers had printing on them, but it was made up for the commercial. I have no idea where the text came from but someone had written a series of simple stories. Now I wish I had taken one of the papers at the end of shooting because I can't remember what it was. One was a story about a prom queen who entered the dance with two machine gun toting thugs. Nothing in it made literal sense and it jumped around a lot. It was hilarious. I am sure the prop person wrote it and had copies made to have identical pages for the commercial.

Nike Commercial - spectator RSA Prod 12/01

I wish I had taken more notes because I cannot remember anything about this job today.

X-Files - Cult member uncovering spaceship in a 2 part series, on top of ship in every shot, FOX TV 2002

Filmed at night in a cold field somewhere in California cow country. We had to park and take a shuttle van for 10 minutes or so into the deep countryside. It was a night shoot so we had to wait until it was dark to start shooting. We watched the cows on a distant hill and argued over whether they were real or plywood props. Finally after several minutes one moved and the question was settled. While I was in the holding tent a girl with long hair looked out the tent flap and the light caught her hair in such a way that I thought that would have made a beautiful photo and at the same time the girl sitting next to me turned and said exactly the same thing I was thinking. We got to walk by two charred skeleton bodies to and from the set. They generated many comments on the prop department's good work. It was very cold and during breaks we would huddle around propane heaters clamped to dollys. This is fairly common for on site night work like this. We shot many scenes that were either not in the final cut of the show or were edited down heavily. In one cut scene a baby was supposed to cry. The primary female cult associate had to make a baby cry for a shot of him crying. She never had to make a baby cry on purpose before so everyone tried loud noises or yelling 'no' but the baby would not get upset and cry. Finally she started fake crying herslef 'waaaaahhh' and the baby picked up and started crying on his own. The tools(crowbar/hammer) we had laying out were rubber but looked real even up close. The spaceship was made of a foam like material. By the end of shooting it was filled with dimples where people stepped on it or hit it with their knees. We had to be careful not to step on the windshield because it was not supported well. When you see the cult leader drilling into the top of the spaceship he is actually drilling into my dime. The foam ship was too delicate to actually drill so we put a dime under the drill bit. The sparks that appeared in the final show were not there but were added in post production. The bright light that is shown when the cult leader climbs into the ship was not done in post but is a very powerful xenon lamp that was filmed with heavy smoke effects. When we were stepping on the ship everyone was going counter clockwise but I saw the camera was pointing across the ship so I stepped clockwise taking up the only open spot. Everyone behind me had to continue counter clockwise. I was now directly in front of the camera. I show up twice, once for an instant with the other background and once blurry next to the cult leader. This is after I was called in at least 3 times for additional shots since I was standing next to him. In the end all of those shots were so tight that no one but the primary showed up. Before filming we had to have our wardrobe approved and be dusted with fullers earth(fake real dirt) to look dusty as if we had just dug up the space ship. It was a total waste of time. You never see close-ups of even in focus shots of any extra except for one girl that appears for 1/2 second and then it is her face so the fake dirt on her clothes and her selected wardrobe was never shown. Hollywood seems to spend a lot of time with details that never make it into the final show. I was chosen for this because the casting director thought I looked

Amish? I have had people guess Irish or English but never Amish. That is how these things work with casting directors. Their decision making process can be all over the map. The truth is anyone of average height and average build would have filled the part(as well as any other background part) equally well.

MCI Commercial - John McKenroe, spectator, HSI Productions, 1/17/02

This is the one where Mike Piatza(sp?) is on a tennis court and finds out he is playing against John McEnroe. The commercial was filmed in one full day(8 hours or so) starting at 6am. They were very specific on what the spectators of the tennis match should wear and would not let anyone wear their coats(even though it was chilly) during filming. We could put them on between shots and stuff them under the chairs during filming. They also moved everyone around so every camera angle would look like the place was full of people. When I saw the final commercial I was surprised at how much time they wasted with pointless stuff. No one in the background can be seen clearly, it would not matter if they had sweaters or coats on because it would look like a small blur among the few people that were actually almost seen in the shot. They used 80 extras but could have used cardboard cutouts and 10 extras with the same result.

Carnivale - HBO Series Pilot, Townie, 1/27/02

This was filmed at night behind an amusement park. It was very cold and we filmed well into the early morning. They used actual vintage 1930's clothing on the extras. Apparently this is not uncommon. Many costume companies have actual vintage clothing for such scenes. One scene was of the Moroccan Girls of Mystery or something like that. Two unfortunate girls had to parade on a stage while we 'onlookers' gawked at them and the barker tried to entice us to pay to see the show inside the tent. Of course there was no tent just a stage out front and a sign with a curtain. It was about 35 degrees and these girls had to stand up there looking warm in skimpy outfits. I was cold and I had sweats on under my vintage 1930's clothes. They must have really been cold.

Franklin Templeton - Subway rider, Commercial, MJZ Productions 2/2/2

I am actually seen in this one. As the camera pans around the city it drops into a subway and I am the one that gets up and walks in front of the camera. During filming they had several 'franklin templeton' newspapers with the logo printed on front or back to give the director some options. The director wore an orange jumpsuit and a wooden necklace with a photo of the Bagwan. Rather unusual but he seemed to be a real nice guy, very professional and intelligent. Our subway car was actually half of a car on a trailer. The movement was made by a big guy sitting on a 4x4 leveraged under the edge of the car. He would sit on it and bounce when they called action. Hollywood magic.

"24" - Fox TV with Keifer Sutherland, crosser, flower buyer, political rally attendee. 3/02

Keifer Sutherland is about 5'6" which is my height, I expected him to be taller. I did several walk-bys as he was shot talking on his cellphone in that urgent way he does. After we shot the footage for the day we went indoors and picked up a lot of generic campaign and speech footage to be shown in the background during the show for future episodes. That was rather fun and free form. Since there was no sound and we had no lines it was a lot of truly meaningless conversation and pointless speeches about nothing. It was funny to see the actors talking about whatever popped in their head. I wore my black boots with my suit because, from experience, I knew no one will ever see my shoes. What is the first thing wardrobe said? Right, they said "Are those the only shoes you brought?" They gave me a brown pair of dress shoes. What is the one thing that was never on film? That's right, my shoes.

Bank of America - commercial, MJZ Productions, sidewalk walker on street 3/02

Not my favorite commercial. We stood on a sidewalk for hours waiting for someone to call action over the radio so we could walk 20 feet and they could yell cut. Then we would go to our start positions and do it again. We did this from 7pm until 5am on a closed off 4 block area of downtown LA. It was cold and we had to stand for a long time while a butcher chased a guy into the street with a meat cleaver over and over and over. The police had the streets blocked off but even at 2,3,4,5am people were walking down the sidewalk where we were working and mentally disturbed homeless people were also walking around. Some were annoyed that we were in their usual sleeping places. The crafts services table where we have coffee/cookies was less than amazing. It was far away and we could not break so it didn't matter much. TV often does not have on site crafts services as good as commercials. Crafts services may seem like a perk when you work a regular job without it but in this business it is more important and can make a big difference in everyone's attitude. When we took a lunch break around 1am we did get a good meal so catering services came through. There was a big water truck there to keep the streets wet. It looks better on camera when the streets are wet. Close to camera the butcher chased a guy into the street and traffic stopped just in time to avoid hitting him. Stunt drivers were in those cars. I thought some of the stunt people were a little less than professional so they must have picked up a second rate stunt company for this one.

Bank of America - 06/02
Boxing ring with desks commercial. I was a photographer and audience member. There were two desks in the ring and someone trying to finish his taxes before the other guy finished with the bank's system I think.

Captain Morgan's Rum - 06/02 Smillie Films
This was a Baseball commercial where I was in the audience. I later found out that during a break after the very first shot when everyone went to the holding area while the camera crew setup for the next shot, a ditzy girl asked the person in charge of casting if she could go home now thinking the day was finished, this was maybe 1 or 2 hours into a contracted 10hr job. The casting director said "Sure, if you don't want to get paid". So later after

the job was finished the casting company started counting up vouchers(what you have signed and turn in at the end of a job just like a time card and what EVERY background actor knows you turn in before leaving) and one was missing. The ditzy girl walked off and took her voucher, oblivious to the obvious fact that she was the only person leaving and not bothering to have her voucher signed, just expecting the world to keep revolving around her it seems...... The casting company paid her anyway because the representative did say "yes" even if it was a qualified yes. The ditz was never hired for another job by the company though.

RUSH - Cinemax after dark movie 06/02

This was interesting. The first opportunity I had to wear a police uniform. It was an ultra low budget project for Cinemax starring Devon, yes the famous adult film star Devon. I was told to show up at 7pm at the Pink Motel. While standing around in my uniform I apparently made some of the crew nervous. Since my uniform is technically accurate(unlike most extra uniforms that have fake security badges etc) so no one was sure if I was a real cop or talent. They kept whispering to the assistant director asking if I was a real cop or with the production and she told me about it for a laugh. We were in a pink motel with a 1950's Cadillac theme and there were many old Cadillacs parked around the lot for atmosphere. They were not part of the production but part of the hotel. It is also pink and, as I expected, there is a big pink neon sign out front. The building is also pink, did I mention that. I was told we would absolutely finish by 10pm. It sounded great. The reason they thought we would finish by 10pm is because you cannot use blank shooter guns after 10pm in the city. Unfortunately because of that limitation they had to film all scenes that used blank shooters before 10pm and put my scene on hold. It was about 2AM when we finished. It was interesting to see a super low budget Cinemax production. A very small crew, and this is the part I liked, the camera was a Canon XL1. I just bought one for my own projects and they are using one for this Cinemax production. Although it did have a lens that likely cost 3x what the camera cost it is still nice to see a camera model I own in a professional production. After sitting around a couple of hours they had 2 masked men kick open a hotel door and fire shoguns as the 2 targets escaped out the back and jumped in their firebird(to be rolled later in shooting) and escape as a man with an airgun shoots pyrotechnic exploding balls at the back of their car. The director was also the writer/cameraman. There were problems. We had 2 police cars rented and a SUV for the detectives. The lights on one police car stopped working from a wiring short, then other car battery died then the rotating police light in the SUV stopped working. We were down to the closeups so they used a flashlight with red gel for closeups. One of the crew swept it back and forth like a police light across the actors faces and it worked quite well. When you are watching it may look(hopefully) like there are police all over the place but in fact there were only 2 uniformed officers(one is me). We had to keep moving and walking back and forth in the background to appear as if the place were active. During shooting the real police drove by a couple of times and eventually stopped by to talk out of curiosity. I guess you get curious when masked men wielding shotguns start shooting and two police cars with lights going are parked in a lot in your area of responsibility. Devon was supposed to scream when the masked men shot and jump in the car. After three or so takes, she was used to the gunfire so when they fired on the fourth take she forgot to scream, then a couple of seconds later remembered and screamed. It was funny to see the two masked men shooting at her and she just stands there for a few seconds then screams. They had some bad communications too. Someone was watching traffic and supposed to say when it was clear so the escaping car could fly out in the street without stopping for traffic. One time they started shooting when the street was not clear so he got lucky when he drove full speed into the city street and did not hit anyone. For an ultra low budget with less than outstanding craft services, it was one of the best jobs I have been on since I was one of two instead one of 20 or 200 and with a small crew I could get close and watch the camera work, talk to the director without being obnoxious or getting in the way. The director had done something like 5 previous films and he did a good job. I was invited to the premiere party and attended at a club in LA. They gave me a screening copy of the movie there too. We all watched it on the big screen TV. The people there ribbed the director asking him how much the helicopter rental cost. In my scene there was a helicopter sound as if a police helicopter was flying overhead but, of course, there was no helicopter and none was shown on screen.

Die Mommy Die 07/02
This is a feature film starring Jason Priestly and the girl from 6 feet under, whatever her name is. It is something about a woman who kills her famous identical twin and takes her place. I play a police officer at the end as she is being taken away and again I am driving the police car they put her in the back of. The girl from six feet under pulled out my prop gun and played with it while talking to me. I didn't know what to say back, but she was nice. I met Jason Priestly too. The police cars looked like genuine old police cars. Dodge Furys from the late 60's with police radios/lights and push button transmissions. This was a short day, show up at 4:30p and wrap 8:30p, all I really had to do was drive a car down the street a few times as I was taking away the woman who was arrested at the end. I was booked because I had my own police uniform but after I got there they already had 1960's uniforms they changed out the entire uniform after I was hired because I had the uniform. Same story for the other 3 policemen there.

Fast Web 07/02
FastWeb is an Italian Internet provider. I was in the 'box head' commercial(not that anyone in this hemisphere will ever see it). I was bystander and a press photographer but really just another 'back of the head' in a crowd. It was a low end job, craft services was minimal but I did get there early so I ate a nice freshly cooked breakfast with scrambled eggs, croissant and bacon from the crew craft services truck before they said that extras were to eat upstairs where all we had was pretzels and cookies with your choice of warm water or orange juice. They did pay in cash at the end of the day and it was a fairly easy day. We arrived at 9am(I arrived at 7am to avoid morning traffic and I have learned it is better to show up early, you get things like free breakfast) and finished at 5pm for a job that was contracted for 12 hrs. During that time we mostly sat in a conference room only leaving for two relatively short

scenes. Lunch consisted of ham, turkey, or cheese sandwiches(for the vegitarians) an orange and the above mentioned warm water or oj. Weak on some points, but an easy day none-the-less. What other job can you show up, sleep 2 hours, work 20 minutes, go to lunch, sit around and talk over an hour after lunch work another 30 minutes before ending the day and not get fired.

Buick 1950's commercial 07/02 The guy from Miami Vice, Zwytek?, is spokesperson for Buick. We all had to dress in 1950's era clothing and pose as press for the unveiling of a Buick SUV, in a 1950's car show. I am a reporter in the distant back. The props department passed out actual 1950's vintage cameras to several people and they used actual 1950's flash bulbs. It seems to be a good thing that we no longer use flash bulbs because they tended to explode when flashing sometimes and caused at least one burn when someone tried to remove one too soon after it was flashed. They had to shoot each shot several times because they were trying different film stocks for different effects and even a hand cranked camera. It took 2 days just to shoot the scenes in the car show/unveiling. I got paid for a 10 hour day on the second day when we wrapped after 5 hours so it came out quite well.

Sprint Commercial 07/02
This was one of the commercials with the black trench coat guy you see in many Sprint commercials. His real name is Brian. About 60 of us stood on a small set of bleachers that were supposed to be in an observatory(I think) of course we were actually in a big studio south of LAX. We would look at one set of studio lights and say "Ooooooooo" then on que everyone would look the other way at another set of studio lights and say "Ahhhhh" for about an hour or two at a time, then the light colors would be changed and we would do it again. Brian would say his lines and we would all appear to be fascinated while looking at the rafters of the studio roof. We spent about 12 hours oohing and aahing with a walk away lunch(which means they screwed us out of lunch by announcing a walk away lunch in advance of the job) and minimal craft services during the day, just orieos/water/soggy chips. No soft drinks even. Apparently sprint is cutting the budget or someone is just cheap up

the ladder. Fortunately my previous experience paid off, I showed up at 6am to avoid traffic for the 8am call and I was the first to be served breakfast with the crew. Other than the oreo's there was no real craft services for background but the girl working the table was nice, too bad they didn't give her much to work with.

Untitled Harrison Ford Cop Movie -
Looks like my picture in a police uniform may be used in a new Harrison Ford cop movie. Don't know what it is or why they want it but what the heck, I told them they could use it.

7-Up Commercial 08/02
This was a 2 day shoot, both long days. We were parade watchers as a marching band and some floats went down the street with the 7 up guy(Godfreed). He pulls the tab on the big 7up float and it opens up spraying the crowd. At least that is my guess. He just opened it up and a crane mounted slide actually slid it back while everyone ran for cover. The marching band is real from a real high school. Apparently the production company paid off a local high school band department to get the kids. They get uniforms and trips out of the band fund. They also had some clowns, one was a real clown, I believe the others were just extras that could juggle and ride a unicycle, also 2 stilt walkers.

They spend an awfully lot of money on this production only to get stingy at the last minute. The whole production clearly cost a bundle. We shot in Downtown Los Angeles at Hope and 7th Street. I am not sure if being on 7th Street was coincidence or not. They had 2 intersections and 6 blocks sealed off for the entire weekend, 12 hour days too. During the first day during lunch someone called in a phony bomb threat so we had double the normal police there for the rest of the day. For food, well not much, we did have donuts in the morning but lunch was ham or turkey sandwiches. Considering they hired 200 extras, plus several specialty extras, plus a marching band, and a professional confetti blower guy, paid Los Angeles for 6 city blocks and filmed for an extra day that was not necessary(my opinion) they could have sprung for some decent food. They would call us to set, we would wait an hour, then they would say Camera's up, we would all get in place and 20 minutes later everyone would have drifted back to a resting place since it was clear camera was not up and they were not ready, then they would come through again "Camera's up" and again 20 minutes later they would again come through and maybe 5 minutes later they would actually shoot a few shots. It looked like they were making some of the shots up as they went and wasted a lot of time. On the 2nd day we had to show up at 7am but they did not call us to set until 10:30am so everyone could have slept late and came in at 10am. Oh well, thats Hollywood.

Roots - Commercial 8/02
About 7pm I get a call asking if I want to work the next day, during the call the casting directors phone rings and I hear her yell in the background in disbelief. The call time is 4:30am! I say sure I'll take it. Roots is a Japanese coffee house like Starbucks I think. They were using Ewan McGregor(jedi knight). Since we arrived at 4:30, of course, they did not start shooting until about 7. We shot on a Universal back lot that looked like New York city on Universal's New York Street. Next time you see a New York scene look at the curbs, none are painted, ie red for no parking, yellow for freight etc. Also all signs are movable. When you see a sit-com set in NY again, look at the bases of the signs, they will not be in the concrete but on stands so they can be moved. We were warned in advance that the commercial featured rain(fake of course) and lots of it pouring over the streets and cabs. They first asked for Non Union people, union people usually get the choice spots next to the main actor. We non unioners(5 of us) were put on a bus that was crossing the street in a running scene. The bus could have been empty and no one would have ever noticed but they wanted realism. So we shot this scene a couple of times as the bus drove through an intersection each time and then they backed up the bus and moved to another scene. No one came to tell us to go elsewhere so, knowing where we would end up if we volunteered, we kept quiet and sat on the bus waiting for instructions. After a half hour or so the bus driver moved the bus, with us in it, to another street out of the shooting. Still no one told us to leave the bus so we stayed. The extras talked. One woman talked about a man she married. She said that after

they were married, she found out he had a wife and child that she knew nothing about and she would likely not marry him if she had known everything she now does. At about 10am we decided to move along before someone did tell us to move which might look bad at this point since we had been waiting a long time. We wandered around the back way to peep around the corner and blended in the outskirts to appear as unused extras for the shot. After a few minutes everyone had seen us and no one thought much of it. Then they stopped to setup for the next scene. We avoided almost an entire morning of standing in fake rain while the union people(who do get paid more) had to walk back and forth in the rain over and over getting soaked. We shot one scene where I was able to stand at the edge of the water spray and broke for lunch at 10:15am. We then shot the next scene and again I was able to maneuver to the edge so I only walked into the edge of the rain every time the directory yelled cut. I made it through the entire day with only a mild sprinkling and spending most of the morning on a cozy warm bus. With a 4:30am call time none of us were too enthusiastic about standing in the rain anyway especially when they said my trench coat could not be worn since it was black(which is what was originally requested). The bus driver was a professional. He worked for a company that only rented buses to film companies so he drove the buses to locations and made sure they worked. They had about 100 buses in their stock.

One girl there walked up to him and said "I have a crush on Ewan McGregor". The bus driver said "really" thinking she had said "You-and-McGregor" so he asked who is this McGregor guy, thinking this strange girl just confessed a crush on him, whom she did not know, and some guy named Mcgregor. It was cleared up quickly but a funny event. They did not skimp on food though. We all had a full breakfast and for lunch there was steak or shrimp(or both if you wanted it). This is the first time I have had New York strip on New York Street in in Hollywood CA. Every 60 seconds or so a tour group in an open 4-section bus would drive by on an adjacent street and take pictures of us at work making film history.

Verizon - Can you hear me 9/02
This was one of the 'can you hear me' guy commercials. We went to a ranch north of LA where they setup a small fair complete with ferris wheel. The stilt walkers were the same people from the 7-up parade commercial. The morning was just us looking busy as they sweep the camera over the crowd, but for the afternoon they needed people for the ferris wheel and I immediately saw the appeal of that, sit down for the rest of the afternoon instead of standing and get to ride a ferris wheel. I immediately volunteered but they wanted Union people, then they had trouble finding any and I was 'in' with the wrangler so he told me to pick someone I wanted to ride with and get on the ferris wheel so I picked a pretty girl and it turned into a good day.

Burger King order sign 9/02
We were the audience on a fictional Steve Harvey(comedian) show where he interviewed the BK order sign(voice by Adam Selzer). Both of them were there in the studio. Steve Harvey had to get up at 4am for his radio show, then we started filming after noon. Extras arrived at 12:30 and the first thing they did was give us lunch. Not bad when you show up for work and your first responsibility is to eat a free meal. For the first 6 hours we sat as the audience just for the benefit of the comedians as they improved lines to see what came out. Most of it will never be on tv, not even HBO. From 8pm to 11pm they actually shot the audience reaction scenes. Steve Harvey seems to be a real nice guy. He talked to the audience a lot and to lots of individuals. The director 'Reg' was also very cool, he just sold a pilot to Fox and got the news of the sale while we were on set. Steve Harvey kept everyone laughing through the day, it was a pretty good day overall.

09/02 AFLAC Insurance Headquarters Productions
The great Kreskin hypnotized an actor on stage to turn him into a chicken. We were assured that it would make sense in the final commercial. The commercial was also filmed in a Spanish version. Kreskin and the actor could not speak Spanish so they read from cards. The duck is actually several ducks and several puppets. Each does something special, one walks, one with a nice bill is

used for closeups, etc. I was in the audience near the edge so no one will see me if they see anyone other than the primary actors.

09/02 SeaBiscuit movie

Apparently a new movie called Seabiscuit is in production. There will be a 1930's race track scene with about 500 people. I really was not interested in doing the job and made an excuse to get out of it, but the owner of the casting company called me back to see if I would do it so I agreed. The first thing I had to do was wardrobe. I had to drive to LA to be fitted for a 1930s suit. We were told to wear a suit so we would look nice and professional to the fitting anyway. After they put me in a suit, that looked almost exactly like the one I already had, and a shirt that will look no different on camera than the one I already had, 1930's shoes and hat they took a photo and cut my hair. This actually worked out well because I needed a haircut and I did get paid for the 2 hours I was there, just not the 2 hours of drive time to get there and back. It was not really worth showing up for minimum wage so when they called back to say they wanted me to go to a second wardrobe review, I passed and said I was booked. Then a few days later they called me again and this time wanted me even without the second fitting. It was a decent day where we stood on a train platform and waved at the star as he arrived on the train.

Sony Playstation PS2 10/02

Sony was putting together an industrial video, that means it is either for internal use or for trade shows so I doubt it will be on TV. We were movie theater audience members watching a 'foreign movie' which was actually shot earlier that morning in LA and edited while we waited. The main character had to work his way down the row of people an just block the screen with his arms and two drinks when nudity appeared for a moment before switching to the ps2 commercial. It was a pretty easy day, drop by at 3pm finish by 8pm, didn't even have time to eat anything but a sandwich at craft services. If you ever see it, that is the back of my head in the foreground very clearly eating popcorn from a cup close to my mouth.

Out of Timers - Disney Pilot 11/02
Either the director or a producer saw my photo and wanted me specifically to be Napoleon in this new Pilot. I guess they thought I looked like Napoleon. I will appear in a photograph with a little girl. Apparently stuck on her wall in her room. Her hero is Napoleon so maybe they will call me back if it is picked up as a series.

Home Depot Commercial - 11/02
Santa in a mall. I was a mall walker. We got paid to walk up and down the mall while they shot Santa talking to some people.

Tostitos -Little Richard commercial 11/02 Headquarters This might have been an easy day but I had other things to do and just wanted to wrap it up. We started at 5:45am, which meant I left home at 3:45am to get there an hour early. This turned out to be smart because I got a hot breakfast before they announced that non-union people were not supposed to eat from the truck. While waiting to start shooting I was standing around with everyone else and the Assistant Directory walked up and introduced himself and asked my name. I thought that was odd and he did not do it for anyone else, just me. For lunch all we had were turkey or ham sandwiches, not very good and a downturn in a bad day. We sat ready for 30mins that morning in the cold before they decided they didn't need us so we went to holding until 2PM! Basically no one did anything even after showing up at 5:45am. We were finally finishing the shots at 4:30p and I noticed the AD talking to someone and pointing at me. I figured the missing piece of the puzzle was about to fall in place. I was placed next to the primary actor and had to nod when he talked to me. So I may get a big pay upgrade if I am not cut out of the final commercial and be on tv where someone can recognize me. Little Richard was there but his scenes were the ones they shot in the morning instead of us.

Animal Planet - 12/02
Animal planet had a promo about a dog show and needed a big crowd. There were 6 of us. We were filmed against a green screen to be digitally multiplied into a large crowd. Funny to walk onto

a green screen set the first time, the corners are rounded and everything is evenly lit so there is no horizon, just solid bright green all around you. It was an easy job, hired for 6 hours but it only took 4 and still got to eat with the crew plus met some nice people.

BurgerKing - 12/02
A woman presents the new 99 cent whopper. We were a crowd gathered for the unveiling of a big blue smurfburger. They didn't call it that, but we did because it was blue so they could key out the blue color in editing. I am sure Burgerking has nothing against Smurfs.

Miller Light - 12/02
Miller light is putting together a commercial with basketball players. We were contracted for a 10 hr job in Long Beach(far south for me) so I had to leave at 4am to get there early enough to eat with the crew and before anyone else showed up. After a fresh warm breakfast I checked in to find that we were to be an audience for the final seconds of a basketball game. The director did several rehearsals and set everything up carefully, after a few takes they shot once more this time firing confetti in the air. We broke for lunch. Disappointing to find we were stuck with sandwiches but during lunch we were told it was a wrap, so we were through and could leave, full pay and we didn't have to stay the full day so not a bad trade off for a sack lunch. I learned that you cannot be shown or appear to be shown drinking alcohol in an alcohol commercial. Our Miller Light bottles had water in them but we were told not to turn them up as if drinking while filming.

MTV - Urban Legends - New show to replace Osbournes around mid Feb 03, 12/02
This was a pretty good job, more pay than usual and it only took maybe 1 hr of actual shooting. I was supposed to be an alien in an urban myth recreation but they wanted to use the girl that was the hiker for another scene so they put the mask on her and I was the hiker. Then we shot another where two of us as police officers arrested the alien. It should be the 3rd episode of the season. We shot in a park, no big crew, just 4 crew and 3 actors. After we shot the scenes

we ordered pizza and had a little picnic there in the park for lunch.

Cisco - Ballroom 12/02

Not a great day but okay. I got this job because I had a tuxedo. Cisco has a commercial upcoming where they award a 20k$ check to fictional Ben Morris but he is not in the ballroom, or maybe he is, we will just have to see when it comes out of editing. Instead of feeding us(250 of us) they paid us all $10 each in cash and let us walk to any of the local downtown LA fastfood/restaurants. I usually complain about walk-away lunches but when they pay you $10 and you are in downtown LA it is not such a bad arrangement.

Radio Shack 01/03

This was with 'The Boz'. He seemed like a nice guy. I didn't talk to him but several people had him sign balls and give autographs. I am sure those radio shack checks would make me jolly too. At first it seemed like it might be a long day. I arrived early, no one was there. No breakfast. We were told to look for the signs. No signs. I found the parking lot based on my directions easily. Then I was told, no we have to park in the other parking structure, so I moved, then they say no, the other lot is the one for us, so I move back, then they say, no, we need you parked in the middle aisle, so I move again. Now the crew is late because they were shooting late the previous night and their call time was changed but not ours so we wait until about 10 am when they were ready. We walked around the Boz as he passed 2 girls in an outdoor restaurant(actually faked outside the Universal Raddison Hotel). I am right behind him with a pretty girl. They shot the same scene several times and when it was time for lunch they said wrap. So that was it for the day. We were contracted for 12 hours and it only took about 4 hours. A pretty good day.

Sea Biscuit - movie 01/03

After I got home early from the Radio Shack commercial I got a call from Bill Dance casting. I was surprised because he called me for Sea Biscuit once before and I flaked on him after I got my wardrobe. It just was not worth the small paycheck to drive out there again. When I went for the wardrobe fitting I got paid $23, it cost me about $15 in gas plus 5 hours total including driving time. I called and told them I couldn't make the shoot, which is a no-no after a fitting, and they would have to find someone else. So now only a month or so later they call me again and see if I can go in next day with no fitting, using my own suit. Which any man there could have done and it would have made no difference since everyone had hats and overcoats. I have no certain plans and after a good day I say sure, I'll do it. Only after that do I find out it is a 5:30am call time and there are 300 people on this call. I have to get up at 4am to get there on time. I had to drive THROUGH Fillmore 20 miles to go to a meet location just so I could ride a bus back to Fillmore. I did not know where the shoot was. Well I do show up, they give me a green ticket. I don't know why but I am rushed through wardrobe approval to get my hat and overcoat, hair, makeup, to set. I use a police break-away tie(velcro) for extra work since it is easy to put on and take off without tying and you often have to do that when changing. I was told to wear a light colored shirt that was not white. What is the first thing I have to do? Change to a white shirt. The wardrobe person also had no idea what a break away tie was. I thought that was unusual for someone who works in wardrobe which outfits police uniforms to not know what a break-away tie was. Now it is 8:30 am or so and cold. We were promised a breakfast. When we got there I headed straight for the breakfast line, I was the last person served and among the first to arrive so no one else got breakfast and I thought I wasn't because someone said the line was for union only and asked if I had a union ticket, I said sure and pulled out the green ticket not sure if it was union or not. They accepted it and I got the last scrapings of eggs and pancakes. Good. So now i have the ticket of power and I am full so I go to holding. We wait maybe an hour before going to a fabricated train station to see a horse and a train. I could have stayed home and they would not have known the difference. Since I wore my own suit(exactly like every other dark 1920's suit there) I had to stand in the back where I could not be seen. The problem with this is that I could not be seen. I was never on camera in any way so I was not actually needed. Then we go back to holding for a long time, they call for people in suits, I start out, no not green ticket people, I go back, again this time I am picked but when I get to set they say 'sorry no green ticket people' I go back, it is lunch time and I see the very first people in the crew getting lunch from a nice barbecue so I jump in line. There is one extra in front of me and no others. I get a nice BBQ chicken breast and pasta. Sit down in the nice tent with table cloths and we eat. Several minutes later it becomes clear that we are not supposed to be there because only crew are coming in. We finish and leave. As I get back to holding I see what the real meal was, a cold ham sandwich and chips. Well now I really am feeling superior. I have the green ticket that gets me out of work, I have had a hot breakfast that no one else got, I had a hot lunch that no one else got. Then they called for the green ticket people and took my hat for someone else. Now with no hat I can't be in the shot at all. After a while they took the green ticket people to set and gave me another hat, then behind the set, then to holding again without ever using us. The rest of the day I sat in holding waiting for the clock to expire. If I had known all this in advance I would have parked in Fillmore, left after I arrived and come back when we were finished, no one would have known the difference. It was almost lousy but at least I got overtime to make it even out as far as pay.

Geico - Dodger Stadium 1/03
Geico has a commercial in the works that takes place in Dodger Stadium. There were about 250 extras and they moved us from place to place so it would appear that the stadium was full when they composite the shots. It was a full 10 hr day moving from seat to seat and we were used all day. Only a box lunch but there were 250 people so can't expect more. I did get to walk on the field and the grass and sit in the high priced blue padded comfortable chairs behind home plate, as well as level 1 and level 2 several times.

Miller Light - Evander Hollyfiled 2/03
Evander Hollyfield is in a boxing ring as a man has a fantasy that he is fighting Evander but the guy gets his head knocked off. This was a 2 day shoot but it was interesting to see how they filmed the head.

Brian McNight music video 2/03
I touched Brian McNight's chest! Well I am sure some people out there might think that was fascinating although I didn't know who he was until I was called for the video. This one should be out March 25 2k3. The basic idea is that he is singing about cheating on his girlfriend and she is killed while he is away from the house cheating on her. The ski mask guy could not hold his hands up in a threatening way because if he did then MTV would not accept it because it was 'too violent'. Hmmm. He can hold his hands down to his sides and walk into a womans bedroom with a ski mask and it is OK but if he does the same thing with his hands up then it is not acceptable for tv? Anyway, I am one of the crime scene cops, the only one wearing a hat. We showed up at 6pm, waited around until 10:45pm, shot one scene in one take and that was the end of our day they sent us home after that 30 second shot. We had to prevent Brian Mcnight from crossing the crime scene tape. We were not really there long enough to expect a meal but still got freshly fried mozzarella sticks. It was a pretty good gig, full pay for a day and we spent most of our time comparing uniforms and talking police stuff. When leaving, craft services was packing up and some rice krispy treats were strewn on the table, I picked up a couple and asked if I could take them, the crafts services guy grabbed a hand full and stuffed them in my pocket and another until I had them all. He was very nice. I also met some people I knew from 'the biz' but had not met before so it was an interesting job. I didn't take my new digital camera this time because I was not sure it would be appropriate since I had not worked for this company before but after finding out the house was once owned by Frank Sinatra during the Rat Pack days and seeing the view from the mountains as well as the shoot itself I regretted not taking it. I expect to take it from now on whether or not I use it.

Miller Genuine Draft - 02/03 House of Usher Prod
A guy gets coffee on his suit, steps in dog poo, then a pretty girl drives by and splashes him with water. We were the people on the street. Filmed in downtown LA with one lane was blocked off, any cars in the background are real people doing their own thing and not actors. They used something in a can for the dog poo, I would

guess it was some type of chocolate baking icing or something. It was a short day and all we had to do was walk back and forth. I may be in some of the scenes, I tried to place myself prominently at the start and during the splash. If the full thing airs it may be funny because one second I am walking away and the next I am walking behind the main character again.

Motorola Bouncing Balls Commercial - 2/03
A black Mercedes loses control in an intersection and a truck carrying round balls turns over throwing colored balls all over the road as a man with his camera phone captures the event. They blocked off the intersection and connecting streets in downtown LA all day. Shooting was delayed because apparently Saturday is the preferred day for crane helicopters to be used. Two of them were in use on the same block and one was right above us. The cameramen used Canon XL1s cameras, no film at all. They also used roller blades to get fast moving shots. Someone late for work drove past the police blocking the road and around the barricades but when he turned and met the next policeman who had been radioed about the guy he went for his gun and the guy stopped. Not too smart to run around a barricade.

Mountain Dew, Code Red - 02/03
Mountain Dew has a cherry flavor called Code Red. We were 300 spectators at a basketball game where a fan actor was to run on the court and knock the ball away when the mascot goes for a layup. It was contracted for 12 hours but we finished in 10 and got a surprisingly good meal. No box lunches, but a good cooked chicken buffet style with pasta and rice and deserts as well as all the Mountain Dew Code Red we wanted, they even let people take home some cans after the shoot. They moved us around to make it look like more people were there. During lunch the extras and crew got to shoot some hoops on a court used by the Lakers.

Jet Blue - 03/03
Arriving airline passengers from Jet Blue. Most people were wearing blue with a married couple arriving from Vegas. One of the primaries was a mafia type actor who drops a wad of cash. He

is really from Brooklyn and used to be friends with Paulie (one with wings in his hair) on the Sopranos back on the east coast.

Steamer Iron Infomercial 03/03
I was an audience member for a new infomercial selling a Steamer Iron. It is a plastic steamer wand in the shape of an iron. The main guy doing the commercial was John with the red suspenders, he does many so you have seen him before. He does 3 or 4 per year and that is all he does. He lives in Scotland and is actually English. It was an 8hr day, paid in cash, a little skimpy on the food but pizza is better than ham sandwiches and we knew it was a cheap production in advance. They tried different versions because they were unsure if they were going to offer 2 of the units or 1 and some extra junk. Paige was the girl, she also does many infomercials. Both were really nice people.

Judging Amy - 03/03
I was called directly for this show. Although I rarely do TV, Central Casting wanted a priest so I accepted. When the main characters(siblings?) are walking down a hall, just before talking about how their mother is dealing with the loss of a fiancée, I am a priest walking down the hospital hallway behind them consoling a girl. It was a short day, we were wrapped before lunch and it was a small call.

Guardian - 03/03
Another TV show. Before I got home from the Judging Amy show they called me again, which is very unusual since I rarely ever hear from Central Casting and then to get 2 calls in 2 days is very strange. They usually rely on people calling in and they have thousands of calls every day from people begging for work. I never call them. I had nothing else I 'had' to do so I accepted since the Judging Amy show was interesting. Guardian worked on the Sony studios lot in Culver City. After I got there I found out the call time had been moved from 7a to 8a so I had an hour wait. Craft services was meager, but they had something at least. Typical TV level food. There were donuts in the morning and a nice cake and brownies in the afternoon, so nothing to really

complain about. I am accustomed to more variety though. For lunch it was a 'walk away' but before lunch they did have fast-food chicken sandwiches at craft services so we were not totally screwed out of a meal. It was a small call maybe 15 people. We were office workers while the main characters talked about taking a vacation in a cabin and choosing a couch. We started at 8a and wraped at 9:40p so it was a long day but not bad, for TV. The principals seemed to be nice too.

Monk - tv series 05/03
I was called to be a City Official for the burying of a time capsule on the show. At the ceremony they pay homage to the fictional towns oldest man. I never saw the main character. It was a short day 2pm-7pm with about 30 minutes in front of the camera just before the sun went down.

Enbrel Psoriasis treament - MJZ Productions 06/03
Call time 10:30am, breakfast to order was available, we waited until 11:30 then went down an escalator, then up, then down, then up the stairs, then down, then up/down/up/down and wrapped at 2pm. A short day and we were contracted for 10 hrs.

AT&T Airport commercial 09/03
We were part of a background crowd for an airport commercial where a little girl in a soccer uniform meets a man. There were actually 5 or 6 little girls and they shot the same scenes with each of them to pick the best one in editing. It was filmed in the LA convention center, not an airport but it really looked like an airport when they added the signs, security and car rental counter.

Qwest - Decks 10/03
My first job as a SAG member. There were about 20 of us playing office workers to promote Qwest's yellow pages type information book, Decks. A guy sits on the shelf and answers questions while we were background and stood in the line to get to him.

Fidelity - Airplane 10/03
7am we show up for a 10hr contracted job, about 8 we sit in a mock

up of an airplane, several takes later we break and at 11am they let us go. We sat in the plane while a boy and his father 'flew' over a blackout and the only building that could be seen was Fidelity.

Halls - ballgame spectator 11/03
We were contracted for 10hrs starting at 6am for a Halls throat lozenge commercial. We go to a football stadium where a guy with his two 'sons' are attending the game. He is yelling and dressed up for the occasion to the extreme. After 4 hours they have the crowd background shots they need and send us home. Another easy day.

Animal Planet dog show - audience member 12/03
We sat in as audience members in the Olympic Auditorium for an animal planet promo for dog shows. All day we sat while they threw confetti on us from the top level, then we moved to another section to repeat the process and everyone oohed and aaaaahed at the dogs.

Angle Driver infomercial - 12/03
I thought this was going to be a bad day, only $70/8hrs but it was a good opportunity to take the day off and watch the making of another infomercial made by the same people who did the steam iron and also with John, the red suspenders guy. After lunch John started talking to the director and they pointed at 'the guy in the blue shirt' which was me, and a few others. They started picking volunteers to test their angled screwdriver. They had a few guys up so I thought they passed me over but later they called me down and asked if I wanted to be a demo person so I said yes. I was teamed with another guy to 'build' a swing set. Fortunately we were 7.9 hours into an 8 hour day so they didn't really expect us to build it and had one already built off stage. We started screwing things together until they called cut and then they brought in the finished set and we said how easy the screwdriver was. For 'volunteering' I got double pay for the day plus a set of the screwdrivers which I can use. I could not believe someone said she did not want to do the demonstration. She missed a chance to be on TV plus the extra pay. Everyone in the audience thought the product was great and wondered if we might get a free sample. They said no. Then everyone's excitement was doused when we

heard the price of $39.95 for the screwdriver attachment. It was way more than anyone expected. We were thinking $14.95 tops.

JZ Music Video 02/04
I received a call at 10pm, they needed someone with an LAPD uniform for a 6am shoot on a Music Video for singer JZ. I said I could make it, so with 10 hours of work to do I finally get to bed at 1am, then get up at 4am to drive to LA. Myself and another actor 'harass' two gang members on the street. The shot is wrapped up by 9am. They keep us for the rest of the day until 6pm without using us, but craft services was great. We had double sirloin steak, shish kebabs, and shrimp was also available.

02/04 Miller Beer for President - Moxie Productions
MillerBeerisrunningforPresidentofbeer,asopposedtoKingofbeers. We were the audience at a political rally where the announcement was made. Good food, your choice of chicken, pork, fish or all 3. I had a red, white, and blue shirt with stars and stripes like a flag but never thought to wear it. If I had, I would have been upgraded.

03/04 Right Guard
We were an audience watching a celebrity golf match for Right Guard Deodorant. The main guy(some sports figure) raises his arms and we all collapse. They had a live squirrel on set. The squirrel was also supposed to collapse. He was trained to fall down.

03/04 The Long Dark Kiss - Stephen Baldwin
They called me for this and said they needed a non-union(half pay) cop and asked if I were union, I said yes and there was a long pause, they were hoping I would jump up and volunteer to work it as non-union, I didn't. Then a couple of days later they called me back and offered me the same job with union pay. This was an independent film with Stephen Baldwin and Kristy Swanson. My scene was with both of them. There was a murder and I was one of the cops milling about in the background. This was shot in a loft. The guy who owns the loft and rents it out as a studio is actually someone who has written a number of crime books. He showed us some of his paperwork for a book he was working on. He was also

a consultant in criminal investigations for lawyers and testified for attorneys. I have since seen him on tv shows as an expert. He is a big guy who wears all black. I can't remember his name.

4/04 Coke bus commercial
On a bus a guy is sitting between two children with balloons. The balloons are hitting him in the face so he pops them with his pen. I was one of the people riding on the bus. We set everything up and the police escorted the bus around downtown while we shot the scene. I think of this when I see a bus scene and know it is done the same way.

06/04 Play Station Golf Commercial Go Films Production, Christopher Guest Director
We stood as golf spectators while a man talked to his caddy and hit a golf ball for a Playstation commercial. It was a short day, started at 7am and finished at noon.

06/04 Infiniti Commercial, MJZ Productions
This was a car commercial for the Infiniti. A long stretch of the street was closed in downtown LA on Saturday. The Infiniti would zoom down the street and they would film it, then they shot along side it with a motorcycle car. We were pedestrians. Steak and pasta for lunch plus overtime pay.

I had many other jobs too. These were just a sample from my notes.

THE END

I hope you have enjoyed this look into the life of a background actor and can find your own success in the field.

You can find more information and stories at my website page just for people who have read this book:

http://www.BackgroundActorSecrets.com/private.htm

www.ingramcontent.com/pod-product-compliance
Lightning Source LLC
Chambersburg PA
CBHW071459160426
43195CB00013B/2162